This book is dedicated to Dr. Page Hudson and
Dr. Thomas Noguchi, mentors in the practice of forensic
medicine and to the role of the forensic pathologist as
an independent and natural arbitrator, presenting factual
information to the legal system in the pursuit of justice.

I would also like to recognize the invaluable contributions
of Joe Cavanaugh, editor, Mark Terry, designer, and
Buster Bodhi Press in the development of this book.

Doctor Arthur Lyons
Medical Examiner

Volume One

By Willam R. Anderson, M.D.

Doctor Arthur Lyons
Medical Examiner
Volume One
By Willam R. Anderson, M.D.

All rights reserved. No part of this book may be reproduced or transmitted in any form or by any means, electronic or mechanical, including photocopying, recording, or by any information storage and retrieval system without written permission from the author and publisher, except for the inclusion of brief quotations in a review.

This book draws inspiration from actual events blending fiction with factual information. Names have been changed to protect the innocent. Real life events have inspired the case studies in this first edition in the series, *Doctor Arthur Lyons, Medical Examiner, Vol 1*.

Published by Buster Bodhi Press
BusterBodhiPress.com

Copyright © 2025 William R. Anderson, M.D.
ISBN:9798999150400
Library of Congress Control Number: 2025914717

Cover and Book Design: Mark Andrew James Terry
Editor: Joseph Cavanaugh
Printed in the United States of America

FOREWORD

Throughout the vast majority of human history, legal judgments have been based upon totally erroneous theories and assumptions that led to preposterous outcomes. These theories have decided whether or not an accused was a 'witch' based upon whether she would float or sink when thrown into a vat filled with water, or burning the hands with a hot iron and determining innocence or guilt based on whether or not the wound of a hand burnt with a hot iron healed properly—an unlikely event in the pre-antibiotic Middle Ages.

Countless individuals, often completely innocent, have been imprisoned, tortured, and even executed because of these 'theories' which appear to be ridiculous to us now but were firmly-held beliefs at the time.

In the late 19th and early 20th Centuries, the focus was on the development of the various scientific methods that would aid in the analysis of data that could be considered as evidence both in the areas of criminalistics as well as the medical sciences. This afforded that information to be used to find and prosecute perpetrators of unlawful activities, as well as avoiding wrongful accusations and, in the worst case scenario, convictions of innocent subjects.

The promise that the introduction of science with its perceived inherent precision and objectivity into the justice system would bring results that were more accurate and equitable has, in many ways, been fulfilled. But because of the human factors that are involved in the process, those hopes may not always be realized.

Since any scientific analysis involves human beings as part of the process, a certain amount of subjectivity is involved both in the gathering and processing of evidence. This subjectivity affects the ultimate interpretations as to what the results mean and is relative to the particular case at hand.

At a crime scene, evidence must be collected and submitted to the lab before it can be tested. If certain pieces of potential data are not gathered because an investigator decides that it is 'unnecessary' because it doesn't fit into some preconceived theory that has been postulated relative to that crime, potential evidence pointing in another direction—possibly to another suspect may be lost when that scene is processed ignoring that 'unimportant' evidence.

During the prosecution of a case, the attorneys representing both sides may choose to ignore, or even attempt to hide, evidence that was collected and analyzed but may be exculpatory (proven innocent) as regards their 'suspect', or even point to another person—deciding that winning the case would be better politically than admitting they were prosecuting the wrong person!

The challenge today is to bring to the attention of the public the potential pitfalls that may be encountered when medical science interacts with the legal system—particularly as the presentation of scientific data is almost expected by jurors in any criminal or civil trial wherein such information is, or should be, available.

Indeed, the attorneys on either side of a case may suffer negative consequences if the jurors feel evidence has either been mishandled or not presented in good faith!

Consequently, it is the duty of the forensic scientist—including the practitioners of forensic medicine—to ensure that this type of misrepresentation, whether inadvertent or intentional, never happens!

The traditional function of the forensic pathologist/Medical Examiner was to deal with deaths that occurred suddenly, unexpectedly, under suspicious circumstances, or as the result of any type of trauma, and to determine the cause of the death, as well as the manner—whether it was a natural death, or the result of accident, suicide, or homicide.

In the best of all worlds, this determination would be made by the Pathologist, based upon the actual autopsy findings, and independent of any outside influences.

The reality may be quite different, however, with the police sometimes providing information of the event that is biased toward their take on the case. The prosecution might insist that the Medical Examiner is part of the prosecutorial 'team'. Pressure can be applied subtly that too many disagreements could have an effect on job security. Elected officials and management staff could also ignore the needs of the office in its routine functions to the point of neglect only to become intrusive when a death was the result of some situation that could provide potential for financial liability or embarrassment for the local political establishment.

This is the quandary faced by many forensic pathologists who, while having strong ethical and moral values and insisting that the truth should prevail, are under the constant specter of potential career damage if they are too forceful in resisting their employer—the local state or federal government—in providing support in medicolegal situations, despite the fact that the science doesn't support their position.

Because he was a stickler for scientific integrity, Doctor Arthur Lyons had, on more than a few occasions, butted heads with the powers-that-be in the local government. This included the administration and the police concerning decisions he had made when the autopsy findings didn't support either the investigator's theory of what supposedly happened to cause the death of the person or persons in question, or the attorney's basis for a criminal prosecution.

In no small number of cases, the clear evidence of injuries uncovered in a second autopsy and medical records analysis that refuted the account of the incident provided by the police—and accepted by the State prosecutor—were summarily dismissed.

The findings of Doctor Lyons, a well-known forensic pathologist whose opinions had been widely accepted when testifying in death cases at the behest of the Prosecution, were not only ignored—but not even acknowledged as being involved in the case!

There is often considerable resistance from the official forensic science community, including the Medical Examiners in a particular jurisdiction, to accept any findings from any outside forensic scientists. This happens particularly when a second autopsy, performed by a competent forensic pathologist, questions the initial determination as regards the cause, manner and mechanism of death.

This resistance was evident in Case History #1, "A Questionable Death on the Treasure Coast: The Case of the Deputy-Involved Suicide," where a second autopsy determined the presence of significant injury to the jaw and skull that had been overlooked during the conducting of the autopsy by the local District Medical Examiner's Office. When provided the data, including photographic evidence from Dr. Lyons, refused to even look at the pictures—let alone admit that they had overlooked a critical finding—one that would have changed their conclusion of "suicide" to "homicide"!

The potential introduction of bias into an investigation that is predicated to rest on substantiated factual data is a well-recognized hazard, particularly when the forensic pathologist is swayed by subjective information provided by law enforcement. This happens often in situations in which the investigators have developed a theory not necessarily based upon facts, and they convey that "soft data" to the pathologist in a way that tends to create a cognitive bias that may well result in an erroneous interpretation of the cause and manner of death.

The "Case Files of Doctor Arthur Lyons: Medical Examiner" provides a glimpse into the everyday activities of the forensic scientist when dealing with both the legal community and the bureaucracy of the government. This is where political pressures are a constant factor to be dealt with when the doctors and scientists are trying to provide scientifically sound data to people that, because of their differing agendas, often prefer not to hear those facts.

Sometimes managers and elected politicians were not above attempting to put pressure on those scientists to modify their scientific opinions to meet the needs of a justice system more interested in convictions than justice.

TABLE OF CONTENTS

A Questionable Death on the Treasure Coast: The Case of the Deputy-Involved Suicide

The Incident 12
Lyons Investigation 21
Exhumation and Second Autopsy 29
Fallout & Official Reaction 35
Resolution 40
Taking a New Tack 47
The Final Outcome 55
Epilogue: 61

Death in the Canal: A Police Execution

The Incident 68
Medical Examiner Investigation and Autopsy 72
Lyons' Investigation 75
Law Enforcement Investigation 81
The Second Autopsy 84
Enter the State Attorney 92
The Cover Up 98
Commencing Civil Litigation 111
The Trial 121
The Verdict & Aftermath 139

The Case of the Angel of Death

The Discovery of a Dilemma 148
A Questionable Cause of Death 154
Pursuing the Elusive Truth 162
The Investigations 168
Solving the Puzzle 173
An Overdose of Reality 181

The Case of the High Profile Suicide

The Incident 186
Medical Examiner Investigation 188
The Forensic Autopsy 191
A Second Look..195
Intervention 202
New Revelations 206
Inconclusive Conclusions..211

About the Author 213

Case Study #1

A Questionable Death on the Treasure Coast: The Case of the Deputy-Involved Suicide

The Incident

"Send help immediately," said the caller on the other end of the phone that was being answered and monitored by the Emergency 911 operator. "My girlfriend just shot herself in the mouth and is bleeding like crazy!"

The voice of the caller sounded high-pitched and staccato as the details were relayed, giving the operator little time to respond but finally pausing long enough for her to ask the caller's location.

"Ma'am, what is your location?" the operator asked. "Please Miss, we can't help you if we can't find you."

"Lady, quit calling me 'Miss'," the caller responded, obviously annoyed but speaking a little more slowly, "I'm not a woman; I am a Deputy Sheriff with the County and I'm trying to report a shooting—of my girlfriend!"

The taped call continued for several more minutes of back-and-forth dialogue between the two with the operator attempting to instruct how to do CPR and getting no specific acknowledgment from the caller as to what, if anything, he was doing to respond to any of the instructions.

Although the caller's responses did little to clarify the situation, it became clear that the victim was female and had suffered a gunshot wound to the head—a wound that the caller almost continually insisted was 'self-inflicted'.

The verbal interaction ended about seven minutes after the call was first initiated by the arrival at the scene of the first-responding law enforcement officers—at which point the caller hung up the phone.

"Well, Doctor, what do you think of that?" Stuart Young, an attorney for the family of the young lady referenced in the call and now deceased, asked as he turned to the pathologist sitting across the table listening to the 911 tape.

Arthur Lyons was a well-known forensic pathologist who, after having served in the capacity of Medical Examiner for many years in Central Florida, had, upon leaving the employment of the State, begun a private practice in medico-legal consultation and autopsy examinations—consequently involving him in both civil and criminal situations. This often included cases wherein the cause and manner of death were in question.

This aspect of his practice was the reason Dr. Lyons was now sitting in the lawyer's conference room listening to the tape from the scene of the death of Karen Cox. Karen Cox was a thirty-four-year-old woman, and the mother of a three-year-old daughter, found dead on the floor of her residence by her boyfriend—a Deputy Sheriff whose gun she supposedly used in the infliction of the fatal wound.

"Arthur," the attorney began, "Karen's family is very concerned about this whole situation, which was called a suicide by the Medical Examiner, but they can't believe she would shoot herself. She was getting ready to leave this guy and had her bags packed. They also say she would never leave her daughter alone like this—and this guy wasn't the father anyway."

According to the accounts given officially by the Sheriff's department, the 911 call from the residence of Karen Cox had been initiated by her live-in boyfriend, Jared Fowler, a Deputy with the Sheriff's department. He had given the account of being in the bedroom down the hall from the living room when he heard a gunshot, and then ran into the living room to find his girlfriend laying on the floor with a lot of blood coming from her mouth and nose.

Fowler met the responding officers and medical personnel at the door and according to the paramedics who arrived simultaneously with law enforcement, he appeared calm—simply pointing to the body of the girl on the floor. It would later be noticed, by Dr. Lyons actually, in review of the incident reports that the responding deputies and colleagues of the boyfriend—had indicated that Fowler was 'distraught and sobbing—barely able to contain his grief over the tragedy'.

The notes from the officers who first arrived and the photos taken subsequently by crime scene investigators showed Ms. Cox laying face-up on the floor with pooled blood around her head, blood emanating from the nose and mouth, her right arm lying across her chest and the left arm extended with a large caliber pistol near her opened hand.

The blood had gathered in a pool that extended about two feet on either side of her head. The neck, chin and cheek areas were obscured by the blood coming from the mouth and nose, so consequently no wound was, at that point, visible to the observers at the scene—although Deputy Fowler had volunteered to the first responders that 'she shot herself in the mouth,' when he met them at the door of the residence.

The victim was fully clothed, exhibiting a small amount of spattered blood on the front of her short-sleeved blouse but none was obvious on either the arms or hands, and there was no blood on her slacks or shoes.

There was an expended shell casing located about six-to-eight feet from the left arm of Ms. Cox, but no other disturbance of anything else in the room. Only the EKG lead placed on her chest by the paramedics showed any alteration of the scene or movement of the body.

It was about three hours later that the Medical Examiner's investigator arrived at the scene, forty-five minutes after the office received the call that there was a gunshot suicide and that someone was needed at the scene to remove the body.

Although the Medical Examiner was, technically, charged with performing an independent evaluation of the cause and manner of death in any circumstance involving trauma as well as any death that was sudden, unexpected or suspicious, the law enforcement people generally considered that he had little to do at the scene of an incident other than simply picking up the body and moving it to the morgue.

Consequently, it was not unusual for the call to come well after the event—sometimes after a significant amount of procedural processing had taken place. This often involved moving the body or even worse, allowing so much time to pass that post-mortem changes occurred that could significantly interfere with the analysis at the autopsy.

After death, the cells of the body immediately begin to break down since there is no longer blood flow bringing oxygen, and this process—decomposition—continues, along with external changes such as rigor mortis.

The changes in the tissues, if sufficiently pronounced, can create difficulties when examined under the microscope because of loss of detail in the cells—so-called autolysis—and that can make an accurate diagnosis difficult if not impossible.

Because of this, it is advisable to get the deceased in an environment of refrigeration in order to slow down these changes. For that reason the Medical Examiners require that they be notified of a death as soon as possible—a requirement that many in law enforcement ignore in order to work on what they consider 'more important,' such as taking photos and checking for fingerprints in areas quite apart from the body.

Although it was clear that the body was not to be moved until examined by the Medical Examiner, often clothing was disturbed and wounds examined by untrained officers in a hurry to determine the injuries. Often this practice destroyed trace evidence on the victim's body in the process.

Arthur Lyons had often experienced some of the difficulties of delays in getting a deceased victim into a suitably protected environment early in his career. One such case involved the wife of the manager of a large grocery store who was kidnapped and held for ransom. The kidnappers demanded her husband withdraw $20,000 from the store's safe. Although the police had been waiting for them when they were supposed to make the pick-up, the kidnappers were somehow tipped off and never showed.

Early the next morning, the wife's body was discovered laying in a vacant lot along with her abandoned minivan that they had commandeered during the initial assault. The police were notified and for the next ten hours they conducted extensive examinations of the van and the area surrounding the deceased victim.

While they were processing the various areas adjacent to the body, the victim lay out in the field unprotected from the hot sun and the high temperature of the day. This allowed accelerated decomposition to take place. By the time the Medical Examiner was finally called to the scene, considerable deterioration had occurred—subsequently not allowing an accurate microscopic evaluation of the tissues in what turned out to be Dr. Lyons' case.

Law enforcement's response to a complaint by the pathologist was met with some controlled derision informing the then-inexperienced doctor that there were much more important aspects to this case than the pathology.

While they seemed to somewhat enjoy the fact that they had upstaged the doctor at the time, it was not so funny later. A critical issue in the trial turned on how long the victim had survived after significant injuries were inflicted. This question was raised by the defense relative to alibis that could potentially exonerate at least two of the accused suspects.

The question was whether she was killed by a gunshot wound to the head immediately after she was abducted from her dining room during dinner and suffered observed trauma at the time, or whether she survived those initial injuries for the period of time before she was ultimately killed.

From the forensic pathology standpoint, if the victim had been injured and survived for a period of time, it would be possible to see certain changes in the body related to the normal responses to an injury.

And although Dr. Lyons admittedly didn't completely understand the legal implications of that distinction—apparently related to which defendants were where and when they were there—nevertheless it had become an important issue in the trial.

When an injury occurs, there is an inflammatory response by the body triggered by the damaged tissues that can easily be observed under the microscope. While these inflammatory cells coming into the injured area do not follow a precise time-line, they don't usually even begin to appear for at least four to six hours after the trauma, and then undergo a progression of cell types—acute, sub-acute, and chronic—that can be very helpful in determining the interval between injury and death. This is an issue that sometimes can be a critical factor in legal proceedings.

Because the victim's body had been subjected to heat for an extended period of time, significant autolysis had occurred prior to the time the body was ultimately placed in the cooler at the office. The microscopic slides prepared from the organs and tissues showed too much deterioration to allow an accurate diagnosis to be made regarding the inflammatory response.

The pathologist couldn't accurately determine if she had survived for half a day or only a few minutes. This led to an acquittal of two of the suspects based upon evidence that they only could have been in contact with her eighteen hours after she was abducted.

The defense argued that the victim was killed immediately, and there was no reliable forensic evidence to refute that theory. The police had decided that their examination of the van was more important than preserving medical evidence and allowed mishandling of the body.

The jury was not convinced beyond a reasonable doubt that she wasn't killed immediately, and therefore they were obligated to find, under their constitutional mandate that a person is innocent until proven guilty, those particular defendants not guilty of murder. The unresolved question was "Did they have the right people actually involved in the abduction?"

After that experience, Dr. Lyons became a real stickler for the proper handling of victims of violence or for that matter any cases. This included elimination of delays, allowing the doctors to fulfill their duties without unnecessary delays resulting from law enforcement activities.

"Stuart," Lyons began to answer the question posed by Karen Cox's family attorney. "It sure looks like it took a while for the Sheriff to let anyone know about this death for sure."

"What do you think was the problem?" the attorney asked.

"It worries me that they were trying to get their stories straight. After all the boyfriend was one of their own deputies." Lyons noted. "You've got to wonder what this guy was telling them?"

Later review of the police account would indicate Deputy Jared Fowler reported that he had gone into the bedroom when he heard what sounded like a car back-firing. He said he immediately left the bedroom and walked down the hall toward the living room.

It was in the living room that Fowler told the investigating officers that he found his girlfriend on the floor in a pool of blood and called 911.

"I could tell she was dead," he told them. "So there was no point in giving CPR."

When asked about the weapon, Fowler had responded, "She must have gotten hold of my service weapon—I don't know how. I thought it was on the hall table in the holster."

The report that followed was, to say the least, sketchy. It basically concluded that Karen Cox suffered from depression and grabbed the gun, placed the gun in her mouth and fired, inflicting the fatal wound.

The Medical Examiner Investigator had responded to the scene, taken some photos of the body and the surrounding area, as well as the hallway and the victim's bedroom. Then he placed her in a sheet and a plastic shroud to protect from the loss of possible trace evidence—a concern not often shared by police investigators who would decide to move a body prior to any such precautions.

In any event, the body of Ms. Cox was eventually transported to the Medical Examiner's office and placed in the cooler pending autopsy examination. An exam would be performed by Chief Medical Examiner Viktor Shevchenko who, while not usually performing routine autopsies himself because of purported administrative responsibilities, decided to take over this case. This was done despite the fact that an initial dissection had already been performed by an associate pathologist in the normal rotation of autopsies in the office.

While this was somewhat unusual, it occasionally happened in high profile cases, particularly when there were some particularly sensitive political overtones—like a deputy sheriff being involved in the death of his girlfriend.

Dr. Shevchenko had received his medical training in the Ukraine and started a second career after having served in the military for fifteen years. He came to this country after three years of post-graduate training in Pathology getting a position in a small Medical Examiner's office in Upper New York State.

Although he gained some limited experience in forensic medicine at that office, he lacked the necessary credentials to take the examination to become certified by the specialty governing American Board of Pathology. Consequently, he was not a competitive candidate for many Medical Examiner offices around the country who preferred doctors that were board-certified in the specialty—presumably because they were better prepared by virtue of their stint in a recognized training program.

There was, however, an overall shortage of physicians willing to perform forensic autopsies, particularly in smaller jurisdictions. There were many situations wherein a pathologist who had not formally trained in medico-legal work would be hired. This was basically the route that Dr. Shevchenko had followed in ending up in an office in a small county on the Atlantic coast of Florida.

The post-mortem x-rays revealed a metallic projectile in the back of the skull consistent with a bullet and was described in the autopsy as being in the posterior occipital area, with evidence of disruption of the brain tissues and possible hemorrhage.

The routine in most Medical Examiner's offices is to take x-rays in any suspected trauma death. This is done in order to both establish if a projectile or instrument of some sort is present and to get a general idea as to the trajectory or directionality of the wound track in the case of a gunshot wound.

Following the x-rays, the body is photographed completely with special emphasis on any wounds or evidences of trauma such as bruises, cuts, burns or the like. These areas also are documented subsequently by the pathologist during the initial stages of the autopsy exam, followed by internal photos of any injuries as might be discovered.

The autopsy report on Karen Cox described a gunshot wound inside the mouth which was reported as passing through the tongue before entering the back part of the roof of the mouth, the posterior palate, passing into the bones and soft tissues at the base of the skull, entering the cranial cavity and striking the brainstem. The part of the brain controlling all bodily functions and through which all nerve fibers pass going to and coming from the rest of the body.

The injuries to the brainstem were described as severe with nearly complete transection, contusion of the adjacent brain tissue, and massive hemorrhage. The combination of these injuries would have rendered the victim unable to initiate any motor activity after the shot, since the pathways from the brain to the body were destroyed.

Additionally, there were a few small superficial lacerations around the corners of the lips indicating that a 'stretching' had occurred. This was due to the expansion of gasses from the barrel of a gun discharged within the oral cavity.

A small laceration was also found on the upper part of the right cheek and above the right eyebrow. No other injuries were reported in the autopsy, and the Medical Examiner ruled the case to be a suicide resulting from a self-inflicted intra-oral gunshot wound.

The Medical Examiner had only taken a few days to make the determination that the gunshot wound was consistent with suicide. Information from the scene, and the presence of soot from a close-range firearm discharge on the surface of the tongue and actually within the muscle itself—having actually been forced into the tissues—was a primary indication of the end of the barrel in actual contact with and pressing against the surface.

The information received regarding the scene was primarily gleaned through information from the Medical Examiner's office investigators, who while supposedly conducting an 'independent' investigation apart from the police, actually ended up in most cases—including this one—simply getting the story from the police and relaying that to the doctors performing the autopsy.

In most instances that arrangement didn't create too much of a problem but potentially biased the Medical Examiner by presenting as 'facts' information that may have only been no more than theories generated by law enforcement.

When it was the average citizen involved, there tended to be little if any scrutiny as to whether the determinations made were entirely objective. But since the subjects usually were not aware of the problem, no effort was made to evaluate any potential errors created.

An entirely different situation could arise however—demonstrating the inherent weakness in this type of independent investigation—when members of law enforcement themselves were involved, usually police shootings but sometimes in situations such as found in the death of Karen Cox.

At that point, the Sheriff's office had a quick press conference indicating that the official findings of a suicide were sufficient to close the investigation and no further work would be forthcoming.

So regardless of the protestations of the family and their legal representatives, there would be no further investigations into the death by either law enforcement or State prosecutors.

Lyons Investigation

Arthur Lyons had been formally retained by the family of Karen Cox to conduct a further evaluation of the investigation conducted by the police and County because of their suspicions that her death was not a suicide as had been initially ruled by the Medical Examiner.

Several important facts had emerged in the six months following her death. They had been relayed to the Sheriff at the time, and included statements by Karen's best friend who had been speaking with her several hours before the incident—a conversation in which she had expressed fear of being injured by Jared. She also had relayed her plans to leave him.

Although a complete autopsy had already been performed by the local Medical Examiner, there were many questions related to the death that were largely unanswered.

The exam had revealed the existence of a gunshot wound within the mouth causing massive injury to critical areas of the brain, but there wasn't a lot of description of the interior details—a situation that was noted by Dr. Lyons when he first looked at the written report.

It was important when reviewing cases to be sure all of the available information was included, with particular attention to hard data such as photos and microscopic slides of tissue samples that the pathologist can actually examine—instead of simply depending upon the reports generated on the case.

"Larry, take a look at these." Lyons pulled up the recently-received autopsy photos while he and his long-time forensic technician Larry Hudson were taking a break during the autopsy of a five year-old boy who had been found dead at home shortly after being seen and sent home from a local hospital emergency room where he had been taken by his parents after having symptoms of the flu for several days.

The boy's death had occurred in a small semi-rural community in Central Florida and because he'd been seen by a doctor the day earlier, the local Medical Examiner declined jurisdiction, whereupon the family sought to have an independent autopsy after the ER doctor assigned the cause of death on the death certificate as cardiac arrest.

It was an inside joke that this was a meaningless diagnosis since everybody eventually has their heart stop when they die—but nonetheless it was not infrequent to come across this on a death certificate, and many times to have a family unfamiliar with medical terminology simply accept this as a definitive diagnosis, thinking it was synonymous with heart attack.

This child's family however realized that there was more to this death than they were being told—particularly since he had just been seen by the doctor less than twenty-four hours before.

There also was confusion as to why the Medical Examiner had declined the case, although Lyons suspected the decision had to do with the fact that the Medical Examiner was actually a pathologist employed by the hospital who contracted with the State to provide forensic services. This was a situation ripe for conflicts of interest, particularly when a death was related in some way to medical care provided by that hospital.

In fact, it was an open secret that that Medical Examiner had been heard to say that he would always protect his employer, and no malpractice suits would ever come about as the result of any of his autopsies. This death certainly had the potential of becoming an issue concerning the appropriateness of the medical treatment that was given—particularly because of the timing!

When Larry opened the skull to reveal a swollen brain covered by milky-grey fluid—clear evidence of meningitis—that potential became reality! The child's diagnosis had been totally missed in the Emergency Room, and the decision to send him home turned out to be a death sentence.

Dr. Lyons knew that reporting this case to the family would most likely result in a medicolegal inquiry and not ingratiate him with either the doctors or the administrators in the hospital. But he had concluded many years before that that situation was just an occupational hazard.

While completing all the paperwork on the child, Lyons had pulled up the photos on the Cox autopsy and was eliciting his usually very observant and helpful assistant's opinion.

"Doc, did you look at these pictures?" Larry responded, singling out a series of images showing the tongue and larynx that had been removed from the victim and photographed with a metal probe placed through the hole caused by the bullet. "The only way the bullet goes in a straight line is if it is curled up like a pretzel—how can that happen? I've never seen this in a suicide!"

"Larry, that's a great call," Lyons responded while taking another look at an image he had only glanced over earlier, now realizing the implication of the positioning. As was often the case, Larry's expertise gained from years of careful observations during an on-the-job education had stolen the show!

The pathologist was well-aware of the fact that Larry should have been a successful physician had he not grown up in a small southern town where he, as an African-American youth, would be effectively excluded from any opportunity to pursue a meaningful education that might have allowed him to pursue a professional career.

If the barrel of the gun had simply been placed inside the mouth with everything in its normal position, the bullet would have simply grazed its surface creating a linear tear.
And in order for the bullet to pass through the muscle itself, the tongue would have to have been forced to the back of the mouth —into a position that would have not only been painful but also most likely have caused her to gag!

"She wouldn't have caused herself to gag; she just would have laid the barrel on top of the tongue and shot!" Larry continued. "Sure as hell don't look like any suicide I've ever seen!"

"I'm a little puzzled," Lyons confessed. "If it's not self-inflicted, why isn't there any sign of a struggle? Did she just let somebody put a gun in her mouth and shoot her?"

"Well, maybe she was unconscious." Lyons did acknowledge that this was a possibility he hadn't seriously considered before but suddenly seemed to be a rather obvious explanation for the seeming incongruity.

"Well, she's got a cut on the right cheek and a cut on the right eyebrow, but neither of those look bad enough to knock her out do you think?" Lyons responded.

"Not really Doc, are there any other injuries?"

In review of the information from the autopsy report, it was apparent that the main focus of the examination was related to the gunshot wound itself with emphasis on the areas of injury to the brainstem and recovery of the bullet—even though it was clear that the gun she had used was the Deputy's service weapon, which he told investigators he had left holstered on the kitchen counter.

There had been a fair amount of publicity regarding the case, and at one point because family had vigorously disputed the determination of a suicide, several local and national media outlets had picked up the story. The media had interviewed many of the involved parties including the Medical Examiner and a Criminal Defense lawyer representing Deputy Fowler, although the officer himself declined to appear on camera.

One of the more interesting interviews from Arthur Lyons' perspective was given by Dr. Shevchenko while being taped by a nationally syndicated crime-story television show. In this particular show, Dr. Shevchenko attempted to replicate the sequence of events by which all of the injuries could have been inflicted when Ms. Cox shot herself—including the lacerations to the cheek and eyebrow.

The Medical Examiner's theory was that the weapon recoiled after she pulled the trigger, subsequently flipping upward with the back sight striking the upper facial area.

During the taped interview, Shevchenko was asked to show the entire sequence at which point he picked up the holstered weapon and began to pull it from the holster—with no success.

There was a safety device in this particular type of holster—widely used by law enforcement—that requires a release be engaged before the weapon can be withdrawn, a safety precaution to prevent suspects from gaining access to the gun during possible physical encounters.

It had been determined through interviews with many who know Karen well that she had virtually no knowledge of firearms, and to everyone's knowledge had never fired a weapon. So, the idea that she would have been able to defeat the holster security, take the gun out and shoot herself was immediately called into question by the interviewer, as the Medical Examiner struggled to unholster the weapon for demonstration.

He never did get it out but was provided a dummy prop at which point he put it near his mouth, simulated firing and pivoted her wounds upward to a position where the rear sight would impact the eye and upper cheek. When asked why the recoil wouldn't have just made the gun move backwards, away from the head entirely, he had no answer—just that his investigation determined it to be self-inflicted!

"That's how I ruled and that's how it's going to stay." was his closing comment.

Arthur Lyons had already reviewed most of the information from the official records of the investigation and autopsy but was more than a little surprised when he saw the video of the interview with Dr. Shevchenko. The two men had little contact previously on a professional basis other than being on the other side in one or two homicide cases over the years.

The obvious difficulties in removing the weapon from the holster aside, the Medical Examiner was seated in front of an x-ray view box showing an x-ray of the skull where the projectile was plainly visible. That same x-ray also showed a small linear separation on the front of the lower jaw that Dr. Lyons didn't remember seeing before in the photos provided by the Medical Examiner.

Upon noticing this, he immediately went to his laptop and opened the file. Sure enough, the separation line—clearly suggesting a fracture of the jaw—was obvious, although he'd been fooled before owing to the fact that blood vessels in the bone easily could be mistaken for fractures using the x-rays alone.

Several photos of the chin had showed no evidence of swelling on the tip of the jaw overlying the area of concern when he had previously examined the photos.

But bruising wouldn't necessarily be found if the trauma had occurred immediately prior to a gunshot wound that essentially stopped all bodily functions—including the circulation that would need to take place for at least a few minutes in order to be seen with the naked eye.

And of course, Lyons had reviewed all the findings, revealing that no detailed examination of that area had been done during the first autopsy, although there was some subtle discoloration of the skin evident on the photos. The doctor speculated that these changes probably should have, in most circumstances, prompted the examining pathologist to make an incision to determine if there was any underlying bleeding.

Examining the scene photos was the next step to be considered, and Dr. Lyons noted that there was an expended shell casing located about six to eight feet from the left arm of Ms. Cox. He had to review several images to get a good perspective of the geometrics of the scene.

"Larry," he asked. "What do you think of this?" pointing to the scene pictures he had just brought up on the screen.

Arthur Lyons, while being a well-trained forensic pathologist, had grown up in a relatively modest but well-protected environment in the suburbs of Christchurch, New Zealand. He was well-acquainted with the effects of gunshot injuries, but not really a student of the use of these weapons "on the street" so-to-speak.

And consequently, he often turned to his very knowledgeable and capable assistant, Larry Hudson, who, in contrast to the pathologist, had considerable and maybe somewhat questionable experience on the street—particularly in the case of shootings—where Larry readily admitted that he had both professional and personal experience.

"Doc, you know the shells come out on the right side when it's fired; how do these guys say she was supposedly holding the gun?"

Lyons laughed, "The position of the gun seems to be a mystery! Dr. Shevchenko went on television claiming at one point that the gun was in a handle up position, trying to explain the injuries to the cheek and eyebrow resulting from impact with the trigger guard as it supposedly 'bounced up' as the gun was fired."

He continued that the Medical Examiner had also opined that it was the recoil of the weapon that created the observed injuries.

The problem with this theory is that if the gun is in a handle up position, the shells would have been ejected to the right side, not the left side—where the casing was found! It was a minor but critical detail!

Arthur Lyons was beginning to appreciate the significance of the discrepancies in this case.

"Well, Doc," Larry offered. "They're trying to come up with something that matches their take on the case. They've decided to make it a suicide 'cause one of their own guys is involved."

"There is a hell of a lot of blood all over," Larry continued.

"You can't even tell where the wound was!"

Larry had just made an extremely interesting observation that Lyons hadn't really noticed. Pictures of the scene were indeed so bloody that it was not obvious where the gunshot wound had been inflicted. Neither he or Larry could tell that the shot was intra-oral, but Deputy Fowler was clear when he told the 911 operator that, "she shot herself in the mouth."

"Great insight, Larry!" Lyons responded. "You should be the pathologist and I should be the assistant!"

The information that Karen had told several of her close friends that her boyfriend would often really lose his temper and she was afraid of him had initially raised a red flag with the family. It was a determining factor in their decision to go ahead with a second autopsy, hoping to finally get closure, even if it turned out that it was a suicide.

Photos of the scene obtained from the Medical Examiner showed a suitcase on the bed partially packed with several carefully folded items of clothing. Interestingly enough, there was no reference to these findings in the final police report of the incident, but it was apparent when reviewing them.

This was to become another point of contention when it was discovered, while reviewing all the photos from the case, that only a few were taken of the bedroom. No comments were made about their significance.

Interviews conducted later with neighbors say that they heard screams from the house immediately preceding what they perceived as a gunshot emanating from the inside, although they were never interviewed by any law enforcement officials regarding what they had heard or seen.

The entire scenario, including the clear inconsistencies, not to mention what appeared to be intentional oversights during the work-up of the case further re-enforced the concerns that they were dealing with a clear-cut cover-up.

Exhumation and Second Autopsy

Attorney Stuart Young had discussed the findings extensively with both Arthur Lyons and the family of Karen Cox. As the doctor discovered increasingly more puzzling and disturbing findings—particularly the irregular shadow on the front of the jaw noticed on x-ray but apparently missed during the first autopsy—there was more and more concern that a second autopsy might be necessary.

Karen had been buried for nearly two years by the time Stuart had called, and although there would probably be some deterioration from being in the ground that long, both he and Lyons felt that there still might be enough evidence to shed some light on the situation.

It was important to recognize that anytime a second autopsy was undertaken, it would be imperative to integrate those findings with the initial examination in order to try to better explain the death.

Although Lyons had picked up on the possible jaw fracture shown on the x-ray, being a very conservative practitioner, he kept his suspicions to himself. Still, he welcomed the possibility of examining the body in the flesh so-to-speak.

To add to the uncertainty regarding Karen's death, the attorney had contacted several of her friends. These friends indicated that she had expressed that she was afraid of Fowler and had decided to leave him on the day of her death.

Interviews with neighbors also were conducted by attorney Young who said they heard screams from the house immediately preceding the gunshot. These neighbors reported that they were never interviewed by law enforcement at all, even though one lady had said she contacted them by phone only to be told that the case had been closed.

At this point it was becoming abundantly clear that none of the officials in the County had any interest in pursuing the investigation of the death any further. As the family quietly arranged for the body to be disinterred and delivered to the local funeral home where the casket would be opened and the examination conducted.

Dr. Lyons and his assistant Larry Hudson had arrived about nine o'clock in the morning at the funeral home. Since the body had not yet arrived from the cemetery, they had a little time to have some coffee and pass the time with several of the funeral-home employees who were mingling about.

Larry as a self-taught autopsy tech and an African-American, almost always had an easy rapport with the working folks at these facilities. They regarded him as 'one of the boys' as opposed to the doctors who might come in to perform autopsies and the bosses at the funeral home.

Therefore, he was often able to ascertain the situation regarding a number of their cases from a different perspective—admittedly often involving rumor, but many times turning out to be more accurate that the official story.

"Doc,' Larry began as they were unloading the casket from the truck and rolling it into the garage on a transport roller. "Rumor has it that this boyfriend killed her and everybody's afraid to say something 'cause he's a deputy sheriff."

Lyons laughed. "Well, Larry, we've been here before you know!" reflecting upon an earlier case in which the pair had been involved.

The doctor was remembering back about six years to a very similar situation wherein they had become involved, as a part of the Medical Examiner's office, with a shooting death in Orlando.
In that case, the victim was the twenty-eight-year-old girlfriend of a police officer. She had died of what had been investigated by his own law-enforcement agency and reported to the Medical

Examiner's office as an 'accidental' gunshot wound of the head, again as in the present case, involving use of the officer's service weapon.

The victim had been transported to the hospital in an attempt to save her life but was declared brain dead shortly after admission. At this point she became an organ donor in accordance with her previously documented wishes and was finally presented to the Medical Examiner about four days after the incident.

Although by law any victim of a gunshot wound came under the jurisdiction of that office, the fact that it had been reported as an accident meant that the body wasn't actually examined until well after the fact. It was also after a number of medical procedures, including harvesting of cornea, heart, liver and kidneys, had taken place.

While organ procurement can be authorized in cases of homicide, permission is usually given by the Medical Examiner only after an initial examination is made and the wounds carefully documented.

This was not done because of the initial reporting of 'accident' by law enforcement. Consequently, when the evaluation was done, the forensic pathologist, who happened to be Arthur Lyons, realized that the presence of the punctate areas of burning on the skin caused by hot gunpowder was clear evidence that the weapon was eight to ten inches away from the victim's head when the gun discharged. This finding virtually excluded a self-inflicted wound.

The situation was further complicated in that some of the areas on the skin had been somewhat altered by the effects of therapeutic intervention. But in any event, the pathologist felt that there was enough preservation to make his ultimate conclusion.

Having already worked for several years with the detectives in that agency, Dr. Lyons immediately called the homicide detective working the case and was told that most of the information used to make the determination of accident came from their fellow officer—the boyfriend of the victim. The case had been closed, even though the detective himself wasn't particularly comfortable with that decision.

"Doc," the detective explained, "I think there is more here that hasn't been looked at, but my boss is telling me that the case is closed—so I can't say anything, or it'll cost me my promotion if not my job!"

It was early enough in his career for Lyons still to be surprised by such a response, but the experience taught him a lesson about the political undercurrents that would often undermine the pursuit of the facts so integral to finding the truth in the justice system. So, when history repeated itself in the present case, he was skeptical—but not surprised.

Meanwhile, the casket containing the body of Karen Cox had been rolled into the garage and opened for about fifteen minutes to allow some of the noxious gases and odors to dissipate prior to actual examination of the remains before starting the dissection. It also, to a certain extent, prevented the odors from permeating the entire funeral home and prompting complaints from staff and visitors.

Upon first looking into the casket it was apparent that extensive decomposition changes had taken place with nearly complete skeletonizing of the facial area, leaving only the hair with portions of scalp attached. The lower jaw was detached and laying in two pieces near the now-exposed bones of the neck, verifying that the changes seen on the x-ray were indeed a fracture—clearly the result of blunt force trauma!

"Somebody really gave her a lick," Larry observed. They were carefully removing the body from the casket, utilizing the cloth lining of the casket as a sheet in order to minimize disturbing the now loosely articulated bones as they transferred her onto a morgue table. "That jawbone is pretty sturdy!"

"I don't think that a fist would even do that much damage," Lyons responded, looking at the irregular line of separation and carefully approximating the cracked pieces. "Something pretty hard and heavy did this—like maybe the butt of a gun."

Larry had also seen the pictures from the initial autopsy and pointed out that while there was no bruising, a hard blow couldn't be excluded. "Doc, they should've taken a closer look at the jaw," he observed. Lyons responded that if the gunshot was inflicted immediately after the blow, there wouldn't be a lot of bleeding anyway since the heart would have stopped, and there would be no blood pressure to result in bleeding.

Careful examination of the fractured mandible did show some reddish discoloration on the surface on both sides of the fracture. This was distinctly different from all the other parts of the bone and strongly suggestive of the presence of blood staining, which would indicate an injury prior to death.

There was a semi-circular hole in the back of the mouth involving the hard palate along with fractures extending in all directions and into the base of the skull. These were all the result of the effects of the gunshot wound, as was expected. Pictures from the first autopsy had shown severe damage to the brainstem in an area that would essentially cut off all the circuitry of the nervous system necessary to maintain movement, as well as cardiac and respiratory activity—in other words almost immediate death.

Interestingly enough there were no fractures of the relatively fragile bones of the frontal portion of the hard palate, the facial bones, or the nose—fractures would have been present if the injury to the jaw was the result of expanding gases inside the mouth from the muzzle blast of the pistol.

In spite of the decomposition that had taken place, there was reasonably good preservation of the rib cage, the skin of the torso, and the muscles of the posterior abdominal cavity—all of which exhibited no evidence of any trauma. This was mostly what they had expected, since the original autopsy photos were relatively complete so far as documenting all areas of the body, were of good quality, and didn't show any bruising apart from the face and head.

As part of the team assembled to perform the examination of the now-exhumed body, Dr. Lyons had called in a forensic Odonatologist to evaluate the teeth, particularly a small chip on the lower front incisor that was recognized in the autopsy photos and raising some concern.

They weren't expecting the bonus that they discovered opening the casket—a previously undescribed fracture to the lower jaw. But this was clearly an area where a forensic dentist could be of great assistance.

There was no soft tissue remaining for direct examination at the time of the exhumation. Lyons had reviewed closely both the descriptions and photos from the initial autopsy, and had determined that apart from the hole in the tongue caused by the projectile itself, and a few stretch marks at the margins of the lips, there were no other injuries to the soft tissues of the mouth.

It was clear that if in the unlikely event that the barrel of the gun had recoiled and struck the jaw with enough force to fracture the bone, then severe damage would have been seen in the relatively-fragile soft tissues of the floor of the mouth. These findings were definitely absent when the reports and photos were reviewed.

An additional finding from the photos from the first autopsy was the position of the tongue, which was photographed with a metal probe in place representing the trajectory of the bullet.

According to the photos the tongue would have been curled backward and basically pressed against the back of the mouth in order for the projectile to have tracked in the straight line expected from a bullet passing through soft tissue.

With the tongue in this position, the victim would have experienced gagging as well as moderate pain from compression of the tongue—a situation highly unlikely if she were to intentionally inflict the wound herself.

"So, it was clear that she wouldn't intentionally force her tongue back and choke herself. She would just put the gun on top of tongue and shoot!" Lyons had informed the lawyer during their conversations. "That just didn't make sense.

"It appears that she was unconscious, so consequently there was no resistance to pushing the tongue to the back of the mouth.".....

Reviewing the autopsy photos had also revealed that there was no injury to the delicate tissues of the floor of the mouth and tongue. They would have been severely traumatized if the barrel of the gun had recoiled after the bullet entered the tongue with enough force to fracture the very thick bone of the lower jaw.

Interestingly enough, Deputy Fowler had indicated that he was not in the room when Karen Cox had supposedly inflicted the fatal wound, but he never accepted the factual evidentiary findings that she most probably had not inflicted the wound.

"You know, Doc," Larry had observed on more than one occasion. "How does the deputy know that there wasn't some dude hiding in the other room who came out and shot her?

"You'd think that he would be going all out to find out who shot his girlfriend?" he continued. "Unless of course he knows full well who fired the shot!"

Therefore, despite the efforts of the Medical Examiner to explain away the obvious findings by seemingly ignoring them, Dr. Lyons concluded, based upon the overwhelming preponderance of the evidence, that Ms. Cox had been struck in the jaw, and probably the right eye as well, with enough force to cause unconsciousness. The gun then was placed forcibly into the mouth and discharged—clearly not self-inflicted.

The next task at hand would be to find someone who would be interested in listening to those facts and taking it to the next level.

Fallout and Official Reaction

The findings from the exhumation confirmed the theory that Dr. Lyons had. This theory applied to the pattern of the injuries found, indicating that there were at least two and maybe three areas of blunt force trauma apart from the gunshot wound—the fracture of the jaw and the injuries to the upper cheek and eyebrow—and that all were inflicted very near the time of death.

He had essentially refuted the theories of the death proposed by both the Medical Examiner and law enforcement, and he had communicated his findings—along with rationale for his opinions to both agencies—receiving no response from either.

It was clear to most observers that Dr. Lyons' findings were complete and accurate, and that the only issue might be whether this was pre-meditated or the result of a sudden act during some sort of altercation.

But the establishment was not in any way ready to accept that one of their own deputies had been directly involved in Ms. Cox's death. After initially ignoring Lyons' findings, they came out aggressively to attempt to discredit him and his opinions.

"Dr. Lyons was just a hired gun, and he was paid to come up with anything that would help the family," was the immediate response from the Sheriff in a press interview in an attempt to impugn the motives behind the opinions gathered from the exhumation.

As a matter of fact, Dr. Lyons had, in this situation, performed the evaluation at no charge owing to the financial situation of the family. Typically an exhumation autopsy would cost in the neighborhood of three- to four-thousand dollars.

When it was pointed out to the Sheriff during that same interview that Dr. Lyons had done the examination pro bono and had received no payment, the response was essentially, "he must be some kind of liberal bleeding-heart, so that makes him biased and we can't trust him."

"Damn'd if you do, and damn'd if you don't," Lyons had laughingly responded. "They'll always try to spin anything that doesn't suit their opinions."

"Politicians," Larry had responded. "You can always tell when they're lying…their lips are moving!"

In addition to attempting a direct assault on the credibility of the pathologist and his findings, the establishment, principally directed by the Sheriff's department, had fostered a campaign of misinformation. This was done to question the credibility of the parties involved, and also to intimidate anyone who may be inclined to come forward with facts about the case—including the neighbors who had initially reported the gunshot and were repeatedly subjected to ongoing questioning related to what they had heard and when they had heard it.

Although they had clearly articulated their stories on several occasions, the questions still kept coming—to the point where many people felt that they were being subtly threatened by those same law-enforcement officers.

As the adverse evidence had continued to mount, the level of intimidation accelerated proportionately.

Suggestions that the family had acted illegally and threats of legal repercussions against them if they went ahead with further actions was stated directly by the Sheriff at a press conference. The Sheriff claimed that the exhumation was not cleared with his office—despite the fact that no such permission or even notification was required to perform the disinterment or the exam.

The propagation of such totally erroneous information, however, was directed toward an uninformed populous that readily digested this 'fake news' as 'gospel'.

Consequently, there was a lot of negative feed-back, particularly through social media, against the family for trying to seek publicity at the expense of their daughter's suicide. Meanwhile, at the same time the social media also disparaged the work of law enforcement, a clear dichotomy in what might pass as rational thinking, nonetheless, it's a prevailing trend on the social media platform!

Interestingly enough, Arthur Lyons had developed a somewhat belated interest in the whole social media scene as it was becoming a force in the dissemination of information—often inaccurate information—but information that, incorrect or not, seemed to have a knack for being believed by the general public.

"Larry," he had bemused while dissecting a partially obstructing, inflammatory-appearing mass in the colon of a fifty-five-year-old woman who had died unexpectedly after three days of abdominal pain, having been sent home from the Emergency Room with medication for menstrual discomfort. "What do you think of all this social media interest in our girl with the gunshot wound to the mouth?"

"Bullshit," was the response. "All this media circus about a little white girl getting shot; if this was a sister, nobody would give a damn!"

Getting back to the case at hand, the fifty-five-year-old woman's death was clearly a concern for her family. Because both the hospital had declined to perform an autopsy and the Medical Examiner had decided against accepting jurisdiction, Dr. Lyons had been contacted to find out what had happened and determine if anything could have been done to prevent her demise.

"Larry, give me a little traction so I can pull up the cecum a little bit," Lyons asked as they were beginning the dissection of the abdomen. "I need to get some exposure."

As Larry pulled up on the bowel that was clearly inflamed, a large amount of purulent fluid began to drain from the now-obviously infected appendix into the already inflamed abdominal cavity.

"Well Doc," Larry laughed. "You got your traction; now what?"

The diagnosis was now obviously an acute appendicitis which had not been recognized as being the cause of the pain when she was in the Emergency Room several days before.

Consequently, the infection had progressed until it had spread throughout the body causing injuries to all the organs, particularly the lungs. Because it had been left untreated, it ultimately ended up causing her death.

"I guess we know why the hospital didn't want any part of this mess," Larry observed.

"Exactly," the pathologist responded as he opened a Culturette to obtain some of the fluid for identification of the bacterial organism therein. "Too much chance of getting in trouble with the doctors and the administration."

This was another situation with which Arthur Lyons was more than a little acquainted. It was a problem frequently encountered by the pathologist employed by, or under contact with, a particular hospital, who performs an autopsy upon a patient who died in that facility.

If the autopsy happens to uncover mistakes made by one or more of the doctors—such as an undiagnosed infection or unrecognized heart problem—those findings may end up in a lawsuit, if accurately and objectively reported.

Such legal consequences would often result in members of the medical staff involved in the incident to file complaints against the pathologist to the administration. This places that pathologist in the unenviable position of seeming to be working against the clinicians.

From the practical standpoint, the administration regarded the medical doctors who were admitting patients as a revenue source. This is in contradistinction to the pathologists who are viewed as a cost center that generates little if any easily recognizable revenues to the institution. The large amounts of cash inflow generated by the clinical laboratory was usually conveniently ignored and not attributed to pathologists who managed that lab.

Because of this, the hospital pathologists were very reluctant to do anything that might upset the apple cart, since complaints from the medical staff could very well result in termination of contracts and administrative dismissal from their positions. This occupational hazard that was most easily avoided by simply refusing to perform the exam rather than being placed in an ethically questionable position of fabricating results to protect the medical staff.

Dr. Lyons was fully aware of this situation, which he had experienced himself earlier in his career while providing contract services for a medium-sized hospital in the suburbs of Atlanta. At that time, the results of an autopsy he conducted led to a malpractice action against several prominent surgeons and, ultimately, a decision to terminate his contract for services.

After that experience, he had become very skeptical about trusting the results of any autopsy examination performed by the hospital in which a patient had been treated. In no small number of cases, he actually found discrepancies within a report when reviewing the tissues and microscopic slides at a later date—indicating that while the pathologist did manipulate the data to some extent, he or she had left enough clues that the true facts could ultimately be ascertained.

The situation wasn't a whole lot different when it came to a forensic pathologist employed by, or contracting with, a State or County agency to provide Medical Examiner services. His or her livelihood essentially depended upon maintaining a good working relationship with that agency.

If the doctor created too many waves he or she might well be seeking other employment in the near future. While the routine cases involving ordinary citizens didn't usually upset the establishment figures, cases considered high-profile involving some agency of government, as in the case of Karen Cox, would in many circumstances result in pressure being applied to the doctor to come up with the 'correct' diagnosis.

"It ain't a surprise that they won't agree with you about the gunshot case," Larry had observed. "Their ass is in a real bind on this one! This poor son-of-a-bitch would get fired if he came out and agreed with you!"

That, Lyons had to agree, was the unfortunate reality they were facing.

Resolution

The media campaign against both Lyons and the family of Karen Cox, principally fueled by the local law-enforcement agencies—not officially of course, but behind the scenes—had been intended to discredit the findings of the second autopsy. It was at first somewhat effective, but turned out in the end to have the exact opposite result.

Following the exhumation, news of the findings, including the mandibular injury, had made its way to the press. Further, inquiries came from another widely viewed national investigative news program, "Forensic Investigations," resulting in an hour-long production exclusively highlighting the circumstances surrounding Karen Cox's death.

Extensive interviews were conducted with her family members and friends. There also was a detailed interview with Arthur Lyons, who painstakingly went through the findings from the exhumation as well as giving a thorough review of the role of the first Medical Examiner autopsy, and the manner in which law enforcement handled the entire situation.

While the producers attempted to give equal time to all parties, there was little new information added by the police or the Medical Examiner. The boyfriend's lawyer simply denied everything and continued to characterize the investigation as a 'witch-hunt' and Dr. Lyons as a paid 'whore'—irrespective of the actual facts.

Because of this reluctance, much more attention was paid to the previous recorded explanations, particularly regarding the medical findings than probably would have been the case if a new set of interviews had been conducted. But that was Shevchenko's decision, most likely encouraged by the County and the Sheriff.

Lyons had demonstrated all of the injuries, explaining the significance of the positioning of the tongue and the probable mechanism by which the other facial injuries had been sustained. Most importantly, he focused on the fracture to the mandible, emphasizing why the failure to recognize that injury essentially skewed the entire diagnosis, making suicide much less likely!

Social media immediately picked up on the fact that there was a fracture to the jaw that had been either overlooked or intentionally ignored after that nationally televised documentary analyzing the case had been aired. In it was pointedly referenced that, during one of the previous interviews, Dr. Shevchenko had struggled, on camera, to remove the gun from the specially designed safety holster and then fumbled with the explanation of the injuries. But he never once appeared to recognize the mandible fracture that was so apparent in the x-ray showing on the view-box immediately behind him.

To make matters worse, the Medical Examiner had at first responded to subsequent questions that the fracture of the jaw—

one of the strongest bones in the skull—may have occurred when the mouth was being examined during the autopsy. That this opinion was ludicrous was pointed out by Dr. Lyons during the filming of the documentary: "You would need to strike the jaw with a lot of force with a hammer—and we don't need to hit the victim, she was already dead!"

It also had been pointed out that the fracture of the jaw was not noted or even recognized by Shevchenko prior to the second autopsy. He later tried to explain this fact by saying that it was irrelevant to the discussion at hand. When pressed to give any scientific basis for determining that the findings were indeed irrelevant, the response was silence!

This denial of the well-documented evidence was to continue for the next few months, during which there was heightened interest in the case to the chagrin of both the Sheriff and the Medical Examiner. For them, the best thing that could happen would be that the Karen Cox would be quietly forgotten, but this was not to be!

The family of Karen Cox had referred the case to the Medical Examiners Commission, the state agency responsible for policing the doctors who were performing medicolegal examinations throughout the State. They questioned the initial conclusion of suicide and the rationale for not now amending the manner of death in light of all the new information that had recently surfaced—not the least of which were the results of the second autopsy.

It had been pointed out that the jaw fracture was not noted or even apparently recognized by Shevchenko prior to the second autopsy. Later explanations were woefully lacking in any semblance of credibility. This was a situation that was particularly disturbing to Lyons, not so much that an error was made but that the clear evidence was being dismissed as fake news, rather than just admitting an error that could easily occur with any forensic pathologist.

Arthur Lyons, indeed, had admitted on more than one occasion, that his initial evaluation of a case had been erroneous. But as a scientist, he had re-evaluated the data and corrected the errors—a process that was obviously not embraced in the case of Dr. Shevchenko's analysis of the death of Karen Cox.

One of the areas that hopefully would be subject to the review of the Medical Examiner's Commission would be related to the process utilized in the determination of the cause and manner of the death but not necessarily the accuracy of the diagnosis, or whether there were any outside extraneous influences that may have contributed to the final determination.

Although their function as mandated by the existing State Medical Examiner's Law was, at least theoretically, to monitor all aspects of the offices throughout the state, there had been a strong tendency in recent years to avoid any real investigation related to the accuracy or quality of the autopsies, or the doctors conducting them. More often, the focus was on purely administrative details such as whether or not proper procedures were utilized in releasing photos of an autopsy to an attorney representing the victim's family.

While the general public perception was that a governing board existed to monitor the quality of the death investigation agencies, the reality was quite different. The board too often succumbed to the political winds that happened to be blowing at the time, failing to initiate any type of corrective action against the doctors. Often this was despite compelling evidence that they were operating below the required standard of medical and forensic practice.

Because there was significant interest in the death of Karen Cox from not only the family but also the media, and now the Medical Examiner Commission, Arthur Lyons had been requested by the family's attorney to generate a report of his opinions on the death. The request came even though he had already completed the autopsy report documenting the findings and opining that the death resulted from a gunshot inflicted by another, therefore considered a homicide.

The object of this second report was to expand upon the objective findings of the autopsy and render explanations of the conclusions that had been drawn, as well as delineating the evidence backing up those conclusions.

While it was not always his preference to write formal reports in addition to the autopsy findings, Dr. Lyons did agree that in this particular situation, further explanation would be helpful. He thought this particularly in light of the fact that because this wasn't a formal legal case at this point, there would be no depositions or hearing where these clarifications could be put forward.

In response to the complaint submitted to the Medical Examiner's Commission, the issue was addressed at the next quarterly meeting. At that point a three-member committee was appointed to investigate the situation. It was headed by a chief Medical Examiner for one of the counties in the Florida panhandle. His task was to review the records and determine whether or not any policies or procedures had been violated.

Interestingly enough, that Medical Examiner was the lone doctor on the committee. The others were a county sheriff and a prosecutor, both of whom were members of the Medical Examiner's commission. The committee was given the task of determining whether or not the actions of the pathologist in the case were appropriate and the conclusions sound as related to the standard of "reasonable medical certainty." It was unclear, however, how the non-physicians were going to be able to establish that, one way or the other!

In the two or three months that followed the announcement of an investigation into the handling of the death of Karen Cox, both Arthur Lyons and Stuart Young awaited any form of outreach to them from someone involved with the investigation. Lyons had not only conducted the autopsy that discovered the previously unrecognized trauma, but he also had provided two detailed reports regarding his findings and opinions.

From the singular standpoint of conducting a thorough scientific evaluation of the situation, it would seem to have been critical to gather that information, even if they had already decided to ignore it!

"Doc, I told you they were just going to ignore you," Larry offered while again in the middle of another autopsy, during which the Karen Cox case had come up. "You're the last guy on the planet they want to hear from, 'cause you got the goods on them!"

Lyons had to laugh. "You're always coming up with these brainstorms when we're eviscerating bodies. There must be some deep-seated psychological reason for it."

"I just can't figure out why you guys are always surprised when they pull this bullshit," Larry replied. "You didn't really think they gave a rat's ass about what we found in the autopsy—man, they're trying like hell to make you go away."

Indeed, the Medical Examiner Commission inquiry was essentially conducted without any requested input from Lyons at all and was initially discussed very briefly at the end of their next quarterly meeting, which was open to the public. Consequently the Cox family representatives were in the audience.

One of the family members asked the chairman about the investigation as he was about to close the proceedings, causing some visible discomfort from both him and the rest of the commissioners at the table.

"We've been sitting here all afternoon waiting to hear something about our daughter's death," her mother said rather forcibly after standing. "Can you tell us where everything stands at this point?"

After a few anxious moments, the chairman explained that the inquiry was on-going, that many people had been interviewed, and hopefully they would have a finding within the next several months. This resulted in collective smiles from the family members, who now had had their worst fears confirmed: that there was a concerted effort to cover up the death. They knew this went all the way to the top!

Over the course of the next few months, pressure continued to mount on the Commissioners to come up with some answers. There were letters to the Governor, press conferences by the family members and their attorney, and several articles in the press addressing what appeared to be major foot-dragging on the part of the official State agencies.

Two more quarterly meetings went by with little visible action taking place until it was announced that the investigative committee had completed their task. They recommended that the chief Medical Examiner be suspended for one month for allowing the original medical records to be taken out of the office by the doctor who actually performed the first autopsy before Dr. Shevchenko had taken over the case. Additionally, that doctor—the associate Medical Examiner—was to be suspended from doing any autopsies for one year, apparently for taking those records out of the office.

"So, that's it?" Lyons responded on the phone to Stuart Young's phone call apprising him of the decision by the Commission. "No mention of all the stuff that was missed in the autopsy, and nothing about changing the death to a homicide?"

"That's it, Doc," Young answered. "You really didn't think these wimps would actually step up to the plate and challenge the establishment on this?"

To Arthur Lyons the outcome had been all too predictable based upon his prior experiences with many governmental agencies. The political winds would frequently upstage the facts when dealing with situations that made the establishment uncomfortable—not the least of these being when a law enforcement officer was a potential suspect in a criminal investigation.

"Stuart," Lyons replied rather insistently. "Don't get discouraged. We really need to push the issue now!"

"Agreed," the attorney shot back. "The problem we have is 'how'?"

There was always the general perception, particularly by the public, that once an official determination had been made regarding the cause and manner of a death, there would be little if any recourse if the family wanted to dispute the findings. But while there was a well-developed system of stone-wallin in place,

Lyons had learned a few tricks that had been quite beneficial in the past.

And he certainly was not inclined to be timidly conservative in approaching this case now!

Taking a New Tack

During the video taping of the interview with the Forensic Investigations program, Arthur Lyons had developed a fairly good rapport with the producers as well as the lead investigative reporter for the show. He consequently had maintained an on-going communication in regard to the progression of the case.

As the scenario unfolded, it became increasingly difficult to characterize the entire investigation as anything but a widespread cover-up—involving law enforcement, the County administration, and the Medical Examiner both at the local and State level.

There had been some initial hope that an inquiry by the State via the Medical Examiner's Commission would bring the facts of Karen's death to light. But their actions were a clear indication that while they did address the nuts-&-bolts aspect of how Dr. Shevchenko's office had failed from the bureaucratic standpoint, there was no attempt to address the quality and accuracy of the medically related aspects of the cause and manner of death determination.

Generally speaking, medical professionals, doctors included, are subject to many kinds of review processes related to their practices—including by medical staffs in hospital and clinic settings, as well quality of care assessments by their peers in individual and group practices.

For better or for worse, those types of peer reviews have never been a significant—or even an existing—part of forensic pathologists' practices. This resulting in a situation wherein little effort is made to determine the quality of practice of any individual doctor as it relates to the accuracy of their diagnoses.

This particular situation had been an issue that had always interested Dr. Lyons as a potential means to improve the data generated by pathologists in the course of death investigation. This data that often had far reaching consequences, particularly when the ultimate determination might result in someone being convicted of a crime.

It would appear that this type of analytical review would be welcomed by the community of forensic pathologists. In reality, any efforts to establish such a review mechanism had been strongly resisted by that very community, leading to extreme frustration on the part of the small minority interested in developing such a mechanism.

"You know," he had mentioned to Janet Chen, one of the show's producers shortly after the Medical Examiner Commission's findings had aired. "This is exactly the type of case where we need some way to judge whether the doctor knows what the hell they are talking about or not, and see if there's anybody outside pressuring them to call it one way or another."

"What do you mean? There's nobody outside their office who's evaluating these cases?" Ms. Chen asked. "I thought peer review was pretty standard operating procedure in medicine—like tissue committees and hospital staff reviews?"

Dr. Lyons went on to explain that because there had been a tendency over the years—principally on the part of the pathologists—to separate the practice of forensic medicine from the mainstream medical community, many of the safeguards built into most other areas of established practice standards didn't exist in medicolegal death investigation.

"We had spent many hours trying to convince those guys that having a review system would ultimately be beneficial to them, providing other pathologists' opinions to back-up their own. In practice, this would protect them from people putting political pressure on them from the outside! But there was apparently too much of an ego problem for most of them—not wanting anybody watching over their shoulder."

"I don't think the public has any clue that there's so little accountability in the Medical Examiner's offices," Chen replied.

"And it sure doesn't look like the Commissioners are going to do much of anything substantial in this case!"

The conversation between the two had ended with suggestions that this would be an area that needed to be revisited in the very near future. This was in keeping with the policy of the Forensic Investigations show to apprise the citizens with important issues involving legal investigations—not simply a crime report—and setting themselves apart from the usual local newscasts.

Ms. Chen waited only a few weeks before again reconnecting with her now go-to pathologist informing him that they would be considering the production of a series of special investigations that would focus attention upon the functioning of the Medical Examiners in these types of cases. They would try to provide insight into the reality that many of these determinations as to cause of death generally were not subjected to critical review by anyone outside the particular office involved.

Working very closely with Arthur Lyons over the course of the following three months, Janet Chen and her co-producers would put together a show involving two or three cases. These cases, including the death of Karen Cox, would be presented in a one-hour, nationally broadcast production that focused upon errors that had occurred during the work-up of those cases and led to situations wherein the cause and manner of death as determined by the Medical Examiner or coroner were highly suspect.

The planned format was to present a brief synopsis of the case as it had initially unfolded, with input from law enforcement, witnesses, and prosecutors, followed by analysis of the forensic medical evaluations that ultimately determined the course of the case—how the death was ruled, and whether subsequent involvement with the legal system followed depending upon that ruling.

A death ruled as homicide, for example would be pursued by the justice system, whereas a 'suicide' might never progress beyond the point of the autopsy.

It was the actual decision-making process at that crucial point, on the part of the Medical Examiner, that would be the central issue to which this program was directed.

This wasn't going to be just another crime show that ended up convicting the bad guy, so the nuanced context in which these cases were presented required some degree of expertise involved in the discussions. Janet Chen had decided Arthur Lyons was just the man for the job!

"Dr. Lyons," the voice on the other end began—a voice that his caller ID showed was from Forensic Investigations' main number. "This is Janet from Forensic Investigations."

"I can see that, Janet, how are you doing?" was the reply.

"Oh yeah, I guess you can" she replied. "Anyway, I wanted to ask you something about the show. We reviewed the tapes from your interview on the Karen Cox case, and you came across very well, so we thought you'd be perfect to give the forensic discussion on the cases for the new show."

Although initially he had signed on only as a consultant for the show, the more Lyons thought about it, the more inviting the prospect of actually being a part of the action had become, so consequently he wasn't totally surprised when the producer broached the idea to him.

"Actually, I have been thinking about this too," he replied. "There are a lot of cases out there that need somebody to let the viewers in on what's really going on! They think everything's pure and simple like the CSI-type shows—not reality."

"I take that as a go," Janet Chen responded.

"You've got it," Lyons answered. "Send me the contract!"

Over the course of the next two months, Arthur Lyons and Janet Chen were intensively involved in integrating the pathologist as not only a consultant, but actually providing on-going commentary relative to the particular issues being highlighted in each case presentation.

"You know," Lyons had remarked. "This isn't a lot different than presenting forensic evidence to the jury in any Medical Examiner case."

"Agreed." was the response from the producer. "That's exactly how we want to portray this!"

Over the course of his career, first within the governmental-based Medical Examiner system and later as a private practitioner, Dr. Lyons had gained somewhat of a reputation for being able to translate the jargon of forensic medicine into everyday terms. He was able to explain to jurors who, while not necessarily familiar with the intricacies of the science itself, were generally quite capable of understanding the concepts as they related to a specific case—so long as this was explained to them in plain English.

Over the years, he had seen all-too-many so-called 'experts' attempt to dazzle the jurors with their expertise but ended up as being perceived as talking down to them—a situation that in many cases backfired when those same jurors didn't appreciate being treated as dummies.

Consequently, he had always taken on the role of teacher, attempting to impart enough scientifically based information to educate the jurors—at least in the limited context of the case in question—to allow them to use that information to arrive at a decision on their own. Lyons never would get up and tell them that they should believe him because 'he was the expert and he told them so!'

This approach had turned out to be extremely effective in dealing with jurors, so they decided this was the way to go in the program—an initial presentation of the case in a narrative format followed by Dr. Arthur Lyons providing a forensic analysis, ultimately arriving at a conclusion, that would be compared with the actual outcome. That conclusion would be subsequently analyzed as to whether the facts coincided with that official determination.

It took a while to come to the realization that they would have no chance of presenting any of these type cases in any depth unless they devoted the entire hour of the show to a single case. Since they had planned on at least a short series anyway, the idea of focusing on only one case at a time seemed most reasonable.

During the first interview they had conducted regarding the issue of the death of Karen Cox, the focus was more on the presentation of factual data without getting into the area of critiquing the quality of the investigations either on the part of law enforcement or the Medical Examiner.

Now Arthur had much more of a free reign in directing the narrative and wasted little time getting to the issue of the serious lapses that had occurred, particularly on the part of the Medical Examiner. He highlighted how the seriously flawed information provided by the Sheriff's office investigators contributed to the errors on the part of the forensic pathologist performing the autopsy.

By the time the opening introduction—wherein the details of the scene, the 911 calls from Karen's boyfriend, and the comments from the first responders were aired using actual audio recordings to fill in the gaps during the narrative—was complete, the viewing audience had been given an overall view of where the case stood, in real-time, when the Medical Examiner's office first became involved.

At this point, Arthur Lyons began to take the viewers through the process by which a forensic pathologist—in this situation—would begin to work-up the case. He began with the information provided by his own investigators—information that would ultimately direct the doctor in exactly the wrong direction!

"Often the public gets the impression, particularly from watching a lot of the crime shows, that the police investigators are simply 'after the facts ma'am,' and that all the information gathered is accurate and unbiased. In realty neither of those parameters are necessarily true in many situations," he stated.

It was important from the standpoint of understanding how errors can be made during the very first parts of an investigation, and that those inaccuracies may not be discovered and subsequently be carried through the entire legal and judicial process. Biases may affect the initial evaluation at a crime scene with decisions as to what evidence to collect and what to ignore.

Information given to the Medical Examiner may be presented as fact but colored by the opinions of the persons providing that information, particularly in situations wherein the police investigators are eager to make sure the forensic findings comport with their own theories of the case.

The existence of this problem was often dismissed by members of the forensic pathology community, many stating that this type of influence 'could never happen in their offices.' He would usually respond by pointing out that it probably happened, but just wasn't discovered—as this type of influence was often subtle, sometimes even unintentional.

In his capacity as a consultant, particularly after leaving his position as a County Medical Examiner, Arthur Lyons had been exposed to this type of oft-silent bias, when reviewing medicolegal cases—often to a much greater degree than in his previous capacity. Indeed, he had actually come to the realization that he had been the victim of this misinformation on more than one occasion, and simply hadn't recognized the problem.

"Doc?" Larry had asked one day while sewing closed the body of an eighty-one-year-old woman who had died of pneumonia in a nursing home after developing a large decubitus ulcer in her sacral area—the result of laying in one position in bed for too long without being properly cared for by the staff of the facility. "You're always bitching about what they tell you about these cases, but do you remember that case you screwed up by listening to what the police told you?"

Arthur Lyons actually hadn't thought about that particular situation in quite a while, but the details came back almost immediately after Larry had mentioned it.

It happened the first year he was at the Medical Examiner's office, just one year out of training, and somewhat of a rookie in the profession, trying to do his best on every case he was assigned. He was faced with the stab-wound death of a teenager found on the sidewalk near the house of an individual who would later become the prime suspect in the homicide investigation.

The story given by law enforcement was that the stabbing occurred during an altercation close to where the body was discovered, and that there had been several prior incidents involving the two within the past several weeks. These incidents resulted in the police responding to the scene on at least three occasions.

Throughout the autopsy examination, the detectives involved in the investigation were conspicuously present in the room, offering information they deemed helpful to the pathologist in making his final determination.

The problem that Arthur Lyons didn't recognize at that moment, as a relatively naïve rookie in the profession, was that while he was extremely well-versed in the science of the profession, he had virtually no insight into the political undercurrents that were so pervasive in the field of medicolegal investigation.

Initially he bought into the scenario constructed by the detective there in the autopsy room, without giving the science itself a whole lot of thought—particularly the physiological realities that would later become apparent.

Dr. Lyons essentially agreed that the stab wound would have caused enough injury that the victim was incapacitated near the point that he was found—clearly implicating the suspect who lived two houses down—and testified in court to that effect, convinced in his own mind that he'd properly analyzed the situation.

The defense had employed an older, more experienced pathologist who pointed out that the cause of death, following the stab wound that involved the right ventricle of the heart, was actually the result of the pericardium—the sac surrounding the heart—becoming so full of blood that the increased pressure interferes with the pumping action required to circulate blood throughout the body. Death will ensue unless that pressure is somehow relieved.

The critical issue that Arthur Lyons hadn't really appreciated was the fact that the stab wound had injured the right ventricle, which was the low-pressure side of the heart, so it would take a longer period of time for enough blood to flow into the pericardium to cause the tamponade that would actually stop the heart from beating.

Since it wouldn't immediately fill up after the wound was inflicted, it was not only possible, but likely, the expert pointed out, that the victim could have traveled at least several blocks from where he was stabbed to where he was found.

This obvious incongruity caused the jury to have serious doubt as to who was the actual assailant, and found the accused not guilty. With that outcome, upon reflection, Lyons was relieved that his tunnel vision combined with unwisely accepting information from those whose job was to convict someone of the crime, had not resulted in the conviction of an innocent man.

Because the State prosecutors rarely went after another suspect after an acquittal, despite the presence of strong evidence pointing to that other person—evidence that obviously had been ignored during the previous prosecution—the guilty party in the fatal stabbing went unpunished.

This was, however, a valuable lesson for the newly-credentialed Arthur Lyons. It would serve him well throughout the many remaining years of his professional career.

The Final Outcome

The airing of the first episode of Forensic Investigations once again brought the circumstances surrounding the death of Karen Cox to the attention of the public and ignited a firestorm on social media, with many posts being generated. Most of the comments were being directed at what was perceived to be a possible cover-up involving the police and the Medical Examiner.

The public interest was piqued even more strongly than after the first interview because of Dr. Lyons' focusing on the specific problems that had contributed to the erroneously diagnosed suicide and the increasingly clear evidence of the cover-up that had ensued.

Although the family had filed repeated requests to the Governor and the State Department of Law Enforcement that had previously gone unanswered, the notoriety gained by the national media exposure apparently began to make the politicians uncomfortable. The State Attorney General announced during a press conference that they were beginning an independent investigation into her death.

Jared Fowler had since resigned his position at the Sheriff's office and joined a small police force in a rural county in the Florida Panhandle following a series of disciplinary actions. The nature of these had not been disclosed to the public despite the Sunshine Law in the state. The law was designed to increase transparency by allowing the public access to government proceedings and records; although most folks realized it only applied to matters the government wanted to be transparent!

Although the Medical Examiner's Commission was technically a part of the State Department of Law Enforcement, this inquiry was directed toward the establishment of criminality, if it existed, related to any aspect of the investigation into the death of Karen Cox. It was not confined only to the involvement of the Medical Examiner.

Consequently, Arthur Lyons was pleasantly, but not completely, surprised when he received a call from the chief investigator requesting an interview regarding the findings of the second autopsy. The investigator wanted to know how he came to the conclusions enumerated in the report provided to the family and ultimately to the Medical Examiner Commission.

An issue that would arise was whether or not the Commission even looked at—let alone considered—the information provided to them by the pathologist. They hadn't, after-all, ever contacted Lyons with any questions or even acknowledged the existence of the report he'd sent them.

"Doctor Lyons," the voice on the other end of the line began. "I am Paul Guerra. I'm the chief investigator on the Cox case, and I'd like to set up a meeting to discuss your findings."

"Well, frankly, it's good to finally hear from somebody who's interested in looking at the actual data in this case, and I'm hoping it might be you!" was the reply.

The meeting was scheduled within a week of the phone call, and lasted for almost five hours, with the pathologist presenting all the data from both autopsies, including the photos and the actual skull of the victim that had been preserved with extraneous tissues removed—clearly showing the mandibular fracture.

"So, Doc," Guerra inquired. "They never asked to see any of this?" referring to the investigation conducted by the Medical Examiner's Commission.

"That's right," Lyons replied. "They just didn't give a damn about actually finding the facts. They only wanted to get it over with! To hell with the truth!"

Arthur Lyons was keenly aware of the political realities facing anyone conducting an investigation under these circumstances, where the findings might well contradict the official line espoused by an elected county Sheriff, thereby creating a serious potential conflict.

So he tried to somewhat temper his responses—keeping it on a professional scientific level as best as he could. Occasionally, over that long a period of time, he would regress into a short-lived diatribe expressing his frustrations over the entire process—ultimately ending up with a very productive session educating Mr. Guerra to the facts as well as the subtleties of the situation.

"You know, Dr. Lyons," the investigator had observed. "I always thought that forensic science was just a black-and-white process—never guessed there was so much intrigue involved."

Lyons laughed, "You don't know the half of it my friend. There is a lot going on behind the scenes that the public never sees—they think it's all science, and science never makes mistakes!"

Investigator Guerra was clearly impressed with the extent of detail that was reflected in Lyons' report, particularly what contrasted with the original Medical Examiner's autopsy and report.

"You know Paul," Lyons observed. "I'm still a little mystified why they never asked any questions of me the first time. You'd think they'd want to at least look like they were investigating all the possible angles."

"That, Doc, I can't answer," was the reply.

The entire conference had gone pretty well, at least from Lyons' perspective, in that Guerra seemed to be genuinely interested in finding the facts and getting to the bottom of what had gone wrong in the investigation of the incident. The problem would be whether or not the same attitude would be shared by those higher-ups in the chain of command!

Jared Fowler, meanwhile, had retained the same defense lawyer he had initially hired within a few days of the death of Karen Cox, somewhat surprising for a man proclaiming total innocence in the death of his girlfriend.

Predictably, the lawyer had joined in on the attack on the credibility of everyone perceived to be on 'the other side,' even though his client had never been charged with anything.

"You know," Lyons had told the press on several occasions wherein the name of Jared Fowler had been mentioned. "Mr. Fowler claims he wasn't in the room when the gunshot occurred, so how does he know there wasn't an intruder hiding in the next room that came in and shot Karen and then fled?"

"You'd think, as a deputy sheriff, he would be keenly interested in finding out who murdered his girlfriend, wouldn't you?"

The defense lawyer's response to this at first was simply to attempt to characterize Dr. Lyons as a paid whore who would give the family any result they wanted for a fee. Later, having found out that the pathologist had done the autopsy pro bono, not accepting any fee—called Lyons a wacko liberal who couldn't be objective because of his political entanglements.

All the protests aside, the investigation continued unabated, ultimately ending up with a recommendation that Jared Fowler be charged with manslaughter in the death of Karen Cox, and that the investigative procedures utilized by the Sheriff's Department in this case be reviewed. But they declined to formally respond to any deficiencies in the investigation.

Despite the recommendations, the local State Attorney declined to bring any charges against the deputy, citing the lack of sufficient evidence to successfully obtain a guilty verdict as justification for not pursuing the issue. This unfortunately, was a not too rare occurrence in the criminal justice system, which tends to favor those defendants who could afford to mount a substantial legal defense, making the prosecution all the more difficult and raising uncertainty as to the success of a conviction. Larry, upon hearing the decision was incensed but pragmatic. "Well I guess they'll prosecute some poor kid for stealing a Twinkie from a 7-11 store, but won't do anything here 'cause they're not sure of getting a conviction?"

"You know, Larry," Lyons observed. "The idea of declining to prosecute because they're not sure of a conviction is a total cop-out from the prosecutors. They don't even put the case in the hands of the jury. They just don't want to be politically embarrassed because it might hurt them in the next election—for sure if the police are involved!"

"Damn politicians," Larry responded. "Well as the old saying goes, 'You can lead a horse to water but remember what a wet horse smells like!'"

After the family and their attorney came to the conclusion that there was clearly never going to be a criminal prosecution in the case, it was decided to file a civil lawsuit against both Deputy Fowler and the Sheriff's department—alleging a wrongful death and pointing to the fact that the weapon in question was Fowler's service weapon that had been issued to him as part of his employment. The lawsuit further alleged that the investigation into Karen's death had been seriously mishandled, to the point of malfeasance.

The trial actually afforded Arthur Lyons his first real opportunity to present his findings and opinions in a public forum. Although he had performed the autopsy that found the previously undiscovered fractured jaw that completely changed the complexion of the case and issued a report that contradicted the official manner of death, none of this had really been widely circulated except through the social media channels.

There had been a strong push, from both law-enforcement officials and the Medical Examiner Commission, to limit the extent to which this case came into public view. Though it was all potentially public record, there was a recognition that the public wouldn't become too involved if they hadn't even heard about the case.

This approach had worked for many years, and in many cases, so it was no surprise to either Dr, Lyons or anyone else on the team. The strategy, though, had been seriously undermined by the advent of social media, whose contributors had become the scourge of those trying to cover up the death of Karen Cox.

"Dr. Lyons," Stuart Young began the questioning. He had outlined the crux of the case and the defense had simply utilized the strategy of denying everything, and since the pathological findings were the essence of the case in the opening argument, Dr. Lyons was the lead-off witness. "Can you tell the jury how you happened to become involved in this case?"

"My first involvement was actually with the family when Karen Cox's mother contacted me about doing a forensic evaluation of her daughter's death. It had been ruled a suicide and the mom felt that there were too many unanswered questions to simply let it go!" Lyons responded.

He then continued to explain to the jurors the entire sequence of events through a series of questions and answers between attorney Young and him—despite the defense attorneys' periodic interruptions with objections that the pathologist was giving a narrative and not responding to the direct questions. This tactic is employed frequently in an effort to confuse the jurors, but it is one that often backfired when the jury felt the defense was not allowing them to hear the whole story.

By the time he finished the testimony, Arthur Lyons had gained not only the attention, but also the confidence of the panel. After hearing arguments from the defense, they rendered a verdict of wrongful death and awarded the family 2.5 million dollars in damages—including punitive damages against the sheriff's department in particular.

The outcome of the trial was the lead story on the local news for two days, with several reporters initially broaching the question as to why this was not being investigated from the standpoint of a criminal prosecution. The story suddenly and inexplicably vanished with at least two reporters being reassigned to other departments in the midst of their reporting on the Cox trial, effectively terminating the coverage.

"You know, Doc," Larry had remarked after taking notice of the fact that the story had effectively been squelched. "They're too busy reporting on a couple of poor Black kids selling a little pot to care about this shit! It makes the cops look good that they're fighting crime and all that bullshit while the real criminals just keep on keeping on!"

"Well, you're partly right," the pathologist replied. "But these guys did start to report on this case and all of a sudden, everything stopped dead in its tracks. Sounds pretty suspicious to me."

It actually was pretty obvious to everyone involved that the County and the Sheriff had somehow intervened in the promulgation of any meaningful way to inform the public of the situation. They were covering their tracks as they had basically done from the inception of the investigation!

"You know, Doc," remarked Larry. "The Cox family actually came out way ahead all things considered. If they'd tried that guy for murder, there probably wouldn't be a civil case at all.
She's dead either way—too bad—but they've got a couple of million!" "Guess I've not been on the street long enough," Lyons replied. "You're learning Doc," was the reply. "You're learning!"

Epilogue

Deputy Fowler was eventually terminated from his position within the Police Department in the small community to which he had migrated. He had hoped to outrun the adverse publicity that tended to follow him, but was ultimately the victim of his own violent psyche. He was later arrested, charged, and convicted of a serious assault on his newly acquired girlfriend when he put her in a coma from which she eventually recovered with serious neurological deficit.

The State Attorney who declined prosecution in the Karen Cox case was defeated in the next election, but his successor explained that the Statute of Limitations had run out on anything but murder, and he didn't feel he could prove that charge.

And Arthur Lyons and his trusted assistant had moved along to other cases, all the while realizing that justice was often elusive but at least had a fighting chance if you can get the truth out!

Arthur Lyons was no stranger to these types of shenanigans involving the governmental agencies, particularly when controversial cases arose. These cases, almost by definition, would involve some actions, such as police shootings or in-custody deaths, wherein the County would almost invariably have, at least potentially, some degree of liability exposure.

In these situations, there was often pressure applied to the media, be it the editors at the local newspaper or news directors at the local radio and television outlets. The aim was to significantly direct the reporting so it would be viewed in a light most favorable to the politicos even if it required manufacturing the 'truth.'

During his time as a county Medical Examiner, there were more than a few instances where a death occurred at one of the local 'high profile' tourist attractions. When there was a question related to a death of a patron while on their properties —whether it involved one of the venues such as an amusement ride, or simply on the property—the Medical Examiner's investigation was met with significant resistance from not only the entity involved, but also the County political establishment as well.

Arthur Lyons had become keenly aware of this seemingly reprehensible behavior early in his stint as a county employee, when a series of deaths had occurred on one of the more popular amusement rides over the course of several years.

Although there had been no specific correlations drawn regarding any relationships between these seemingly unrelated events, it was apparent to Lyons. While evaluating the case presented to him on a Saturday morning while he was taking a call, he realized that this was a situation that needed more scrutiny than had previously been undertaken.

The case involved the death of a sixteen-year-old girl in apparent good health. She was found unconscious at the end of high-speed roller-coaster ride, well-advertised as being the fastest in the county with many hairpin turns and rapid changes in speed and direction.

Since the death occurred in a theme park within the jurisdiction of the Medical Examiner's office where he was employed, it became his task to determine exactly how and why she died. He specifically was told to exclude any relationship to the ride which was accounting for a significant amount of revenue for the park.

The girl had been taken to the hospital after being removed from the cart in which she was riding, but she never regained consciousness. Studies at the hospital revealed severe swelling of the brain—a condition known as diffuse axonal injury—the result of severe acceleration/deceleration forces causing the brain to essentially shake back and forth injuring the delicate nerve fibers in the process.

She was pronounced brain dead after twenty-four hours, and because she was an organ donor, she was operated upon to remove the kidneys, heart and liver. Following the procedures, because of the concern with possible trauma, the case was referred to the Medical Examiner for further investigation and autopsy. At this point Arthur Lyons became involved in performing an autopsy in which no obvious disease processes were identified that might suggest a reason for the collapse, so the findings in the brain became of utmost interest.

Opening the skull, Dr. Lyons noted a severely edematous brain. The normal convolutions of the cerebrum were flattened as they had been compressed when forced against the inside of the skull by the rapidly swelling tissue.

These initial findings, at least to the naked eye, seemed to be hallmarks of injury from rapid deceleration. This would most certainly implicate the ride—and ultimately the theme park for failing to adequately ensure by design that the ride was sufficiently safe as to not incur any such injuries.

Although the pathologist had only been with the office for less than a year, the forensic technologist assigned to assist him was none other than Larry Hudson, who as it turned out would later become Lyons' most indispensable colleague after going into private practice. It was Hudson who brought up the issue of previous similar cases.

"Doc, do you know this isn't the first case like this we've had around here?" Larry approached the doctor a little reluctantly, not yet knowing him well and recognizing that many doctors had serious ego problems and resented a 'lowly tech' telling them anything!

"Really?" Lyons had responded. "Tell me more!"

Even in the few months during which they had only intermittent contact, Lyons and Hudson had developed a mutual respect for each other's knowledge and capabilities. This served to break down most of the artificial barriers that often interrupted the flow of valuable information between members of the staff at various levels.

"Well," Larry continued. "This is the fourth person we've had die on this ride over the last three years, and all of them were healthy and most under thirty. They mostly all went to the hospital but were brain dead, and we signed them out as either pneumonia or heart attack, but they all looked like trauma to me!"

"Do you remember the names of the cases?" Lyons inquired.

"Is a brown bear Catholic? Does the Pope shit in the woods?" Larry responded in his own inimitable style. "Of course, I remember." He proceeded to go back through the computer files in the morgue, coming up with the four cases in a period of about ten minutes.

In order not to create any type of controversy within the confines of his relatively recent place of employment, Arthur Lyons quietly pulled the files on these victims late in the following afternoon after the secretarial staff had left for the day. He was somewhat astonished to find that all the victims had described severe cerebral edema similar to the findings in his most recent case, and all had been found unconscious in the roller-coaster car at the end of the ride or had collapsed shortly thereafter.

"Larry," Lyons turned to his newly acquired right-hand man, who had also stayed late to get a piece of the action and had quietly come upstairs to the Records Room, "This is amazing. They describe the brain as severely swollen in the autopsy but not in the diagnosis!"

Further review of the records indicated that microscopic sections had been taken of the brain tissue in three of the four patients. It was an easy task for Lyons to pull those from the storage room down the hall from Records and examine them himself.

"Damn, Larry," Lyons remarked while peering through the eyepieces of his microscope, "these all have the hemorrhages we see in high-speed trauma, but we can't tell about the nerve fibers without special stains—and it looks like they didn't do any."

"Doc, they really just didn't want to know." Larry responded, pointing out that none of the cases had been ruled accidental, and recalling that he had never seen anything much mentioned on the news or in the local papers about the incidents. "The parks have the County and the press in their back pockets, you know!"

Because the inspection and oversight of permanently located amusement parks had been turned over to local governmental agencies from federal control in the early '80s, there were no longer any uniform standards applicable on a nationwide basis.

This allowed considerable leeway in deciding what was and what was not dangerous.

The obvious difficulty in this arrangement was that local leaders might be quite reluctant to blow the whistle on a localentity that was generating considerable revenue for their community and its government. And that seemed to have become a reality in this particular instance.

Consequently it didn't come as a complete surprise when, after examining the initial microscopic slides on the brain of his own case and seeing the same type of changes—the hemorrhages around the small vessels—his request for the necessary special staining studies needed for making a definitive diagnosis was rejected by the office administrator on the basis of the need to limit expenses.

While Dr. Lyons initially contested the decision, it was made clear that the decision had been made by the chief Medical Examiner, and the issue was closed. There was insufficient evidence to make any correlation between the death and the amusement park ride.

Since the chief in that office had to sign-off on all the autopsies before the cases were closed and released to the public, there would be no further inquiry into the incident by any governmental agency.

Case closed!

Period!

It was these types of activities involving direct political interventions in areas that should have been independent scientific inquiry that led Arthur Lyons to develop a healthy skepticism about the ability of the legal and political actors to embrace the role of an objective forensic scientists in the system. Instead they chose to attempt to manipulate the facts in a way to further their own ends, and in the process they corrupted the mission of the scientist trying to provide accurate and unbiased information to the people charged with deciding guilt or innocence.

Case Study #2

Death in the Canal:
A Police Execution

The Incident

The police sirens filled the night silence in the small enclave of primarily African-American families at the end of a small back street ending at the banks of a large irrigation canal running from Lake Okeechobee to the Atlantic Ocean thru the northern part of Ft. Pierce, Florida. More than twenty cars roared down the street in pursuit of a tan-colored sedan, driven by a Black man later identified as Henry Freeman.

Henry had apparently been driving home from his part-time job at a computer store when, according to later police reports, he had failed to stop when they tried to pull him over for a damaged tail light on his vehicle. Instead of stopping, he drove to his residence, only a few blocks away, driving at the speed limit at least through the neighborhood, according to several residents who observed the incident from their front porches.

By the time Freeman had driven to the end of the road, at least six police cars had arrived at the scene and within a short time that number had swelled to ten patrol squad cars and a Canine unit—all with lights flashing and sirens blasting.

"What the hell's going on." William Deveraux shouted as he ran to his front porch confronting the sea of blue lights filling up his view of the area of the canal. "Who are you chasing?"

"Get your black ass back in the house," was the response from the burly white deputy approaching the front porch with his hand on the .44 caliber pistol at his side.

Deveraux immediately retreated to a position on the back of the porch, but still outside, not willing to relinquish his view of the ensuing events. Still he did not want to be shot in the process.

The deputy, although clearly wanting to exert his authority, decided that he could, even in the heat of the moment, live with this mutually-understood compromise, and he did not pursue the issue.

This compromise, ironically, allowed Mr. Deveraux to have a clear view of the events that subsequently transpired, and gave him the opportunity to record the events on his cellphone, unimpeded by that same deputy!

According to the official police reports, Freeman stopped his car, jumped out and ran into a wooded area that bordered on a large drainage canal leading from an inland lake to the ocean, slid down the bank and attempted to swim the approximately fifty yards to the other side.

The law enforcement account of the incident continued to describe how Freeman began to shout "help me" when he was about a third of the way across the canal. He subsequently was thought to sink below the waters, after which no further sounds were heard.

Law enforcement's initial report from the scene was that the victim had jumped into the water in an attempt to elude the police. But because he couldn't swim, he drowned in the canal despite their 'heroic' efforts to rescue him!

Pressed about the reported gunshot, the initial law-enforcement response was that an alligator had been spotted near the now-struggling man in the water. They had fired into the completely unlighted canal, in a supposed attempt to save from being attacked.

Within a few hours, however, the Sheriff's Department, recognizing the absolute absurdity of this account, issued a press-release that stated that the bystanders had misinterpreted what they thought were gunshots. No shots had been fired—a theory that completely contradicted the first statement that had been generated and was conveniently ignored!

Later accounts from several witnesses who were standing on their front porches, including Mr. Deveraux, would surface, although none of those individuals immediately came forward with any information. This probably was because the deputies had gone to every house threatening the occupants with arrest if they didn't go inside during the events that were transpiring.

Consequently, there was no communication between any of those potential witnesses and the press. Clearly, the law enforcement people weren't particularly interested in their accounts. They seemed unaware that most of the events that night had been recorded on the cellphones of a number of the residents.

The news media arrived at the scene about three o'clock in the morning with a van from each of the two local television station news crews. They set up shop outside the crime scene tape the deputies had strung across the road to create a perimeter around the area where they were working to recover the body.

Although most of the action was down at the bank of the canal, the reporters couldn't get close enough to really see what was going on. But they were noticed by several of the residents who casually strolled over and began to chat with them.

"Hey, did you see what happened?" one of the television reporters asked one of the first people to approach the van.

"Sure did!" responded the late middle-aged Black gentleman. "My name is Deveraux, and I was on the front porch the whole time. Had a real good view too!"

The reporter began to tape the conversation.

"I woke up and heard a bunch of sirens in the distance, and it sounded like they were coming this way, so I went out on the front porch. In a couple of minutes, I saw our neighbor Henry driving real slow down the street toward his house that's on the end near the canal. About four or five police cars were behind him blasting their sirens, but he couldn't have been going more than 20 miles an hour—then he stopped, and the police all jumped out of their cars with their guns out. They pulled Henry out and started beating on him!

I don't know why in the hell they did that, 'cause it didn't look like he was doing anything at all!"

Deveraux went on to explain that Henry Freeman fell to the ground while the officers pinned him down and were punching and kicking him for at least two or three minutes. After that, they grabbed him under his arms and dragged him into the woods next to the canal.

"His legs was dragging and his head was bent down...he didn't even stand up," Deveraux said. "Looked like he was dead!"

The narrative continued, indicating that after about five minutes the officers walked out of the woods alone, got into their cars and drove about fifty yards further down the road. They stopped with their lights aimed out over the canal.

"Did they seem to be in a hurry?" the reporter asked.

"No, they was just walkin' and talkin' on the radio," Deveraux answered, now quickly looking over his shoulder at the two deputies who were approaching him and the reporter.

"I thought I told you to stay in your house," one of them yelled at Deveraux, who now had a look of real concern on his face. He continued to stand next to the reporter and his cameraman.

The deputy stared at the group, and then informed them that these people were witnesses and were not allowed to speak to anyone but law enforcement. He further indicated that the Sheriff's Department would need them to turn over any tapes or videos that might have been made during the interview with this man.

"Anything we recorded is the property of this news station!" the reporter responded. One of the officers, again placing his hand on his service revolver, attempted to take the microphone—not cognizant of the fact that the voice recording was being fed directly back to the television station.

His partner however immediately intervened telling the first deputy that, "We can get all of this stuff later," somewhat de-escalating the situation.

Deveraux in the meantime had quickly headed back to his house before he had had the opportunity to tell the reporter that he, too, had the entire sequence recorded on his cellphone camera video.

Meanwhile, during this interaction, at least a dozen or so law enforcement personnel were on the canal bank in the process of recovering the body. They employed a small inflatable raft, and divers had entered the water about two hours after Henry Freeman allegedly had jumped in while trying to avoid arrest.

"I think we found him," a voice shouted from the darkness. "I've got a rope around him, and we're heading back to shore!"

After several minutes, the raft containing three deputies approached the canal bank with the body of Mr. Freeman in tow, and they pulled him onto the lower bank. While still secured with the rope, the deputies pulled the body up the bank to street level, where he was covered by a tarpaulin to await the arrival of the Medical Examiner.

"These people never learn to swim," joked one of the several deputies at the scene, "Their bones are too heavy...they sink whenever they're in the water!" he continued. "Guess there ain't a lot of water in Africa," the derisive conversation continued, as later documented by several local residents who were bystanders within ear-shot of the activities going on.

It would later be established that Henry Freeman had been working part-time in Florida to help out his sister, but in the Winter months was the owner of a diving school in the Bahamas. He was a trained diving instructor and a superior swimmer—contrary to the 'heavy bones' theory purported by some of the officers on the scene. This particular fact was studiously ignored throughout later press conferences and law enforcement investigations.

Medical Examiner Investigation and Autopsy

The on-call investigator for the Medical Examiner's office that night, John Sweeney, was awakened about four o'clock in the morning by a telephone call. The Sheriff's investigator was calling from the scene where the body of one Henry Freeman was being recovered from the irrigation canal where he had, according to the sketchy account given over the phone, allegedly drowned while attempting to elude police following a traffic stop.

"John," said the voice of Detective Dennis Moran on the other end of the line. Moran was well known around the Medical Examiner's office. "We have this guy that jumped into the water after we just tried to give him a traffic ticket, and it looks like he drowned!"

Sweeney immediately responded, "Dennis, have you recovered the body yet?"

The detective went on to describe the scene where they had lights on the canal, and divers in the water had just found the suspect and were requesting the Medical Examiner to respond to the scene.

"Why does this stuff always happen in the middle of the night!" he muttered to himself. "Do these things ever happen during the daytime?"

Answering his own silent question, the Medical Examiner investigator tumbled out of bed and proceeded to grab his clothes, get into the transport van, and head out to the scene of the incident.

By the time, Sweeney arrived at the bank of the canal, the body subsequently identified as Henry Freeman had been recovered from the water. The body had been dragged up to the top of the rather steep embankment and was laying on the ground covered by a yellow tarpaulin often used by the police in similar situations.

Removing the tarp, he noted that the body was that of a well-developed Black male fully-clothed, laying on his back with frothy fluid emanating from the mouth and nose—a telltale sign of respiratory compromise, often associated with drowning.

The body was cool to the touch, and rigor mortis had begun to develop. This indicated that the death had occurred at least two to four hours earlier, prompting Sweeney to wonder why there appeared to have been some delay between the actual death and when the Medical Examiner's office was notified—contradicting what Detective Moran had told him an hour earlier—but passing it off as a simple miscommunication.

Under existing State law, any death that occurred in police custody or during an arrest or attempted apprehension immediately became the responsibility and jurisdiction of the local Medical Examiner. The Medical Examiner's duty was to investigate the circumstances of the death and determine the cause and manner of that death, specifically whether it was a Homicide or an Accident.

As was the usual protocol, Investigator Sweeney made notes of his observations, took photos of the victim, and placed him on a sheet and plastic shroud. The shroud, subsequently, was wrapped up for transportation to the office for an autopsy.

Using the sheet and shroud provided protection for any trace evidence that might be on the body as well as minimizing the introduction of extraneous material that could potentially contaminate the subsequent forensic analysis. Once the body had been properly packaged, Sweeney placed him on a stretcher and loaded him into the transport van, a process that took about an hour and a half. During that time, he had a chance to observe the scene and have an off the cuff conversation with the investigating officers.

As a Medical Examiner investigator, he was, at least in theory, an independent agent. While he often obtained information from many sources—including law enforcement—nonetheless he was charged with the task of conducting his own analysis of the situation.

It became immediately apparent to him that all was not kosher at the scene of the incident. As an experienced forensic technician, Sweeney was no stranger to situations where some tension existed between the various agencies involved in a death investigation. These were often most obvious in situations involving police officers.

Parenthetically, the presence of a Medical Examiner investigator at a crime scene was viewed by the law enforcement people as pretty routine, as he or she are considered "one of the boys," consequently making them privy to conversations that might not be the case if outsiders were present. This was clearly the case when the officers were discussing the situation during the recovery of the body. There were no shortage of comments reflecting their general feelings towards both Freeman, and indeed, the entire population residing in this predominantly Black neighborhood.

Sweeney arrived at the office about six o'clock AM, just as the forensic techs were clocking-in for the morning shift and beginning the process of preparing the autopsy suite for the upcoming day's work. This day included three autopsies in addition to the body in Sweeney's van.

It was a Saturday, and there were only two techs and one pathologist, in this case Dr. Don Kacey, working the weekend. They essentially performed autopsies in tandem with the doctor moving between two autopsy tables simultaneously as each tech was opening the cadaver and helping him with removing and weighing the individual organs.

This technique was frequently employed on the weekends in order to move the cases along and allow everybody to get out of the office at a reasonable hour so as to not interfere too much with their other weekend activities. It was efficient for sure, but also had the potential of missing something important in the rush to get through the cases.

Don Kacey was relatively new to the job, having finished his training only a few months before taking the job in Florida, and he took a little more time doing cases than some of the "old-timers" who were able to complete an entire autopsy in less than an hour in an uncomplicated case.

The problem the rookie, Dr. Kacey, didn't fully appreciate so early in his career was how sometimes these uncomplicated cases turned out to be anything but uncomplicated!

Lyons' Investigation

Dr. Arthur Lyons had received a call from the sister of a young Black man who had reportedly died following some sort of altercation with the police in this small east coast Florida community. His family was very concerned about the situation—particularly the account given by the police.

Lyons was a well-known forensic pathologist around the country, who after serving as a Medical Examiner in the State system for many years, had gravitated to private practice. In the process he had developed a reputation for being a source for obtaining an unbiased, objective scientific forensic analysis of a situation—and consequently he was referred many cases from both criminal and civil attorneys as well as families concerned with the actual circumstances surrounding the death of a loved one.

In many circles, the veracity of many people involved in forensic investigations, particularly those in the employ of the state or local governmental agencies, was often viewed with considerable skepticism. This was because of the often perceived —and sometimes justified—conflicts of interest that might prevent a proper analysis of a particular situation.

This concern was particularly acute in situations where potential liability existed, usually involving law enforcement activities during arrests or while a person was in custody of a police agency. History had shown that in too many instances, pressures from the higher-ups would interfere with the investigation and the analysis of the forensic pathologist. They attempted to cover their interests—the "cover-your-ass" mentality —regardless of the actual facts of the situation.

For families grappling with questions concerning the death of a relative in police-related activities, reliance on the word of the local law enforcement and government agencies was not a realistic consideration—absent any input from a reliably unbiased source.

Consequently, the services of an independent forensic pathologist, such as Dr. Lyons, were in fairly constant demand. These requests came both from families of patients who died under circumstances that caused concern for their families, and more recently from defense attorneys in criminal cases. In criminal cases questions often arose regarding the completeness and potential biases that might exist when the State-employed doctor performed the examination on behalf of the State.

The possibility of potential bias on the part of the forensic scientists within State agencies had only become an issue in the last few years. A number of studies began to reveal that much of the findings related to forensic science were in reality often based upon opinions—the interpretation of the information—or scientific data, and not simply an analytical compilation of the factual data.

In reality, most all so-called scientific analyses have quite a lot of interpretation involved in the final determinations often are not as black-and-white as the general public is led to believe.

This interpretative component in the perceived 'unbiased' analysis of information would be presented to juries as 'scientific fact'. The presenting parties, usually the State, had little incentive to inform the folks on the jury that these 'facts' might not be reliable, as they were led to believe it was 'science'!

The other side of the coin was that the scientists, while trying their best to be objective, would often experience pressures to make the data confirm with law-enforcement's theory of a case. This pressure could ultimately result in an erroneous interpretation of the data, and in the worst case scenario, could result in a wrongful conviction of an innocent defendant.

As it turned out, Arthur Lyons became involved, almost accidentally, in the issue of perceived or cognitive biases through his review of many cases in his private practice. In these cases the effects of prejudicial attitude on the part of a Medical Examiner may result in erroneous outcomes—in both convictions and acquittals.

Several of the major forensic science societies had begun to look into the issue of cognitive bias and its effect on the accuracy and reliability in the practices of their members, and whether or not there was a potential threat to the credibility—and ultimately the public trust—of their work because of these oft unappreciated outside influences. Dr. Lyons became interested and a vocal advocate of the move to raise the level of awareness both in the profession and in the public consciousness. These concerns ultimately would become a significant factor in how he conducted his practice.

The information provided by Henry Freeman's sister, while a little cursory in its content, did provide the pathologist with some interesting facts that immediately piqued his attention. It was particularly the part about "a diving instructor not being able to swim," resulting in his apparent drowning in the canal!

One of the first instincts he had was to address the obvious—why would an experienced swimmer end up drowning in a body of water that, while having a current of about three miles per hour, was certainly not beyond the capabilities of even a moderately capable swimmer, let alone a professional diving instructor.

Arthur Lyons and his trusted and very-knowledgeable Forensic Technologist Larry Hudson were in the process of opening the body of a twenty-two-year-old woman who had died suddenly after giving birth to a healthy, eight-pound baby when the call came in from Freeman's sister.

The family of the young woman had requested an autopsy after the hospital had failed to give any adequate explanation to the family as to what had happened and had suggested that she had just had a heart attack after the delivery.

"This sure as hell doesn't look like a heart attack!" Larry said as he made the Y-shaped incision across the chest and down the middle of the abdomen." How do these guys think they're going to get away with these bullshit explanations to the families?"

As Larry cut through the thin layer of fat on the front part of the abdomen, the pair saw that there was no blood or even any significant amount of fluid in the cavity. They could see, looking in the pelvis, that the uterus was enlarged and soft as would be expected in a woman just giving birth.

When they opened the uterus after removing it from the body, making a cut from top to bottom, a large amount of blood was discovered inside the uterine cavity—a situation that was certainly not expected. This immediately raised a concern as to the source of all this blood and how that might have contributed to the death.

After draining the blood from the inside of the uterine cavity, a very apparent area of tearing and deep-seated hemorrhage was identified in the area where the placenta had been previously attached. Parts of a large blood clot were visible with the naked eye, indicating that a partial separation had occurred with bleeding between the placenta and the wall of the uterus.

This situation occurs often when amniotic fluid, the liquid that surrounds the fetus during the pregnancy and normally drains out during delivery when the membranes rupture—popularly referred to as "the water breaking"—goes into the bloodstream and ultimately to the lungs. The resultant amniotic fluid embolism frequently means sudden death, and consequently is the main culprit in deaths that occur at or near the time of delivery.

One of the most common causes of the leakage is exactly what they were seeing in this case. The placenta came loose from the wall of the uterus caused a hemorrhage, and fluid entered the bloodstream, ending up in the lung. At that point, the patient experienced a sudden interruption of respiration and died.

"Looks like we've got a diagnosis, Doc," Larry pointed out. Lyons was taking the tissue samples for examination under the microscope—an examination that would ultimately confirm the diagnosis of amniotic fluid embolism.

"I wonder why they called it a heart attack in the first place?" he continued.

It would turn out that the patient had presented to a birthing center nearly twenty-four hours earlier. She was complaining of severe abdominal pain and uterine contractions, but the mid-wife in charge of her case sent her home with instructions to rest, even though she was near-term in her pregnancy.

She continued to experience severe pain and vaginal bleeding, ultimately showing up at the Emergency Room where she went into cardiac arrest and subsequently died. Fortunately, an emergency C-Section was performed, and the baby was successfully delivered.

Later, the interest in calling this death a heart attack would become clear, when the family successfully sued the birthing center for their negligence in not recognizing the problem earlier and taking immediate action.

The autopsy Dr. Lyons performed at the request of the family discovered the actual cause of death, leading to a wrongful death lawsuit that was quickly settled by the insurance company representing the birthing center. The birthing center chose to pay out and avoid the adverse publicity that would certainly accompany a prolonged legal battle, possibly resulting in the facts being presented publicly in a court of law.

Needless to say, Arthur Lyons was not a particular favorite among the defense attorneys representing doctors and hospitals. They were used to a hospital-based pathologist arriving at conclusions that would protect them from adverse legal outcomes —if that pathologist wanted to keep his or her job!

"Well, Larry," Lyons continued after explaining the situation of the drowning case he just started reviewing. "What do you think about this guy in the canal, drowning though he was a professional diver?"

"Was he Black?" Larry questioned.

"Yes, as a matter of fact he was," was the pathologist's response.

"You know those people can't swim!" Larry pointed out derisively. "All those folks that were found in rivers in Alabama and Mississippi in the sixties just drowned when the Klansmen were trying to teach them to swim!"

"Yeah, I know," was the response. "I think we have an updated version of this down on the coast!"

"Driving while Black?" Larry laughed.

"Probably…" was the response.

In communications with the sister of the victim, Jerieka Sanders, Dr. Lyons really had received only a cursory view of the circumstances of the events, but he was able to conclude that there may be some serious issues that needed further investigation.

The Medical Examiner had already performed an autopsy and made a determination that this was indeed a drowning. He determined it should be considered an accidental cause of death —a finding that was clearly not popular with the sister and the other members of her small community, several of those community members had witnessed the entire event.

Freeman's sister had actually contacted the doctor within a week of the incident, and as such, the body of the deceased was still in the cooler at the Medical Examiner's office. The family had not yet made any funeral arrangements, thereby creating a situation wherein a second examination could be conducted without going thru the process of exhuming the body. This was exactly what Jerieka was pushing for!

Law Enforcement Investigation

From the time of the incident, it was clear to most people in the area that the chances of getting to the truth about the death were fairly slim, particularly since the police were involved. There was a long history of violence by law enforcement toward minority communities, which had never resulted in any accountability for their actions.

From the time the body of Henry Freeman was recovered from the canal, law enforcement's response remained unchanged. This was despite the fact that the first press release came out moments after the recovery was made and well before any official examination of the body had been performed or any conclusions determined by the Medical Examiner.

"Mr. Henry Freeman attempted to elude law enforcement following a lawful traffic stop. He fled through the wooded area next to the irrigation canal leading from Lake Okeechobee to the ocean and jumped into the water, apparently trying to swim to the other side. We attempted to rescue him, but we think he was not a strong enough swimmer to fight the currents and subsequently drowned. We were just now able to recover the body, which is in the custody of the Medical Examiner. Further updates will follow when we have more information," was the statement given to those members of the press who had arrived at the scene.

Over the next few days, there was a cursory investigation conducted, basically consisting of photographing the scene and interviewing some of the officers involved in the incident. Official statements were taken and camcorder videos were reviewed, taken from the various police cruiser dash-cams that recorded anything of interest.

Subsequent reviews of these so-called investigations, by Dr. Lyons and the attorneys that the family had retained in an attempt to find answers, turned up very little real information. It was clear though, that using the term "investigation" to describe what went on was a very generous description of what had happened.

Law enforcement investigations are usually billed to the general public as independent, simply because they are conducted by entities that appear to be removed from the officers being scrutinized, such as "Internal Affairs" or in this case, "Florida Department of Law Enforcement." This gives the appearance of impartiality to the outside observer.

The reality, unfortunately, is quite contrary to the actual situation. The agencies are often in close liaison with the State investigators, and certainly with the so-called internal affairs people, who are actually a part of the very organization they are supposedly investigating!

In situations such as those found in the death of Henry Freeman, the deficiencies of this type of system become abundantly clear—if you grade your own test, you will always get an "A"!

This certainly appeared to be the case in this situation.

It was a well-accepted fact in this area of the State that police actions were seldom questioned publicly, particularly in situations involving minorities both Black and Hispanic. This was true even though there had been, over the years, many cases where police involvement in a seemingly trivial alleged offense ended up in a death.

The usual modus operandi in these cases was to hold an immediate press conference explaining, essentially, that the subject had resisted arrest with violent actions, which required the arresting officers to react in order to protect their own safety.

This was followed rapid-fire by a short-term suspension of the officers, with pay, while the investigation was conducted—by the police agency itself. This occurred often before the full details of the incident were determined, including the actual cause of death and the surrounding circumstances.

Typically, as was the case of Henry Freeman, the 'investigation' consisted of obtaining statements from the officers involved and reviewing any video or audio evidence, then issuing reports of the findings ensured confidentiality by not releasing the actual recordings to the public.

Although in many cases there were eyewitnesses to the events, their accounts were seldom sought out during the investigation—and in fact, often suppressed.

It was not unusual for several armed and uniformed officers to suddenly show up at night at a house near where a police-related incident had occurred, asking if anyone had seen anything only after demanding to know if there were any drugs in the house or if anyone was in the country illegally. These were tactics clearly intended to intimidate any potential adverse witness to maintain their silence.

It appeared in this case that they hadn't even asked of any of the people in the neighborhood about what they had seen or heard, let alone thought that any of these people would have possibly recorded any part of the incident on a cellphone. This reflected the general attitude in which the police held a community of even middle-class Black citizens, an attitude that was demonstrated over and over again even when they were involved in the most trivial encounters with that and other minority groups!

There had always been concern in those communities regarding not only the attitudes but also the actual physical make-up of the agencies. Less than five percent of the force was made up of minorities in a community that was only about fifty percent Caucasian.

The suspicion was that many of the White officers harbored significant racial biases and prejudices, although there was really never any way to prove it.

There had been several inquiries by citizens into both the hiring practices of the County law-enforcement agencies and the backgrounds of the people they eventually employed, but these efforts were met with considerable resistance by the higher-ups.

They insisted that such information was confidential and release could endanger both the officers themselves and the public in general.

This argument really didn't make much sense since personal information such as addresses, social security and driver's license information and other sensitive data would be redacted, but items such as prior employment, any complaints filed, records of any arrests, and the like would be available for scrutiny—indeed were generally items considered to be 'public records' and therefore should be accessible.

Several small groups of Black residents in various parts of the County were pressing the administration to release that information, and recently had been able to obtain a considerable amount of information thru internet searches. These searches resulted in suspicions being raised as to whether or not the police officers being hired had previous records of racial discrimination. Some were even to the point of overt involvement with white supremacy groups.

While there was no apparent direct connection between Henry Freeman and any of these actions, the reactions from the establishment seemed to be a blanket response, directed at anyone who happened to fit the profile of being "Black."

The Second Autopsy

Although there was at the time no attorney involved in the case to this point, the sister of Henry Freeman was in direct and constant contact with Arthur Lyons regarding her concerns. She conveyed the information that the body was still at the Medical Examiner facility and requested a second autopsy be performed.

Generally, Arthur Lyons preferred a situation where an attorney was involved, even though the primary interaction was with family in cases involving deaths in police custody or related to a police action. This allowed requests to be made, sometimes requiring court orders, and to be formally made if necessary. But this wasn't the case in initially dealing with the death of Mr. Freeman.

Consequently, he was pleasantly surprised when, after contacting the Medical Examiner's office, there was an agreement to allow him and his team—a team of one consisting of Larry Hudson—to perform a second autopsy in their facility.

"Larry," Lyons began when his assistant answered his cellphone. "We need to head down to the coast as soon as we can to do a case—the one we were talking about the other day."

"You mean the Black mermaid?" was Larry's response.

"That's the one—and don't quit your day-job!"

Explaining that they were going to do it in the Medical Examiner's office, Larry expressed a combination of astonishment and suspicion. He recognized that it was almost too good to be true—and when something is too good to be true—it usually is!

The pair arrived at the office of the district Medical Examiner about ten o'clock in the morning after having driven down from Orlando. They were greeted by the Chief Medical Examiner himself, Dr. Geoffrey Stanton, who was a very competent forensic pathologist who had previously been the head of a large metropolitan office in south Florida before running afoul of the political establishment. He was forced to resign that position—officially to "spend more time with his family."

After that experience, Dr. Stanton retired to a position in a much smaller jurisdiction on Florida's East coast, directing an office with about a 50% smaller caseload. Still, it had about the same level of political interference experienced in his previous position.

Interestingly enough, Arthur Lyons had been recruited for the position ultimately filled by Stanton prior to his taking the job. But he was put off by the insistence of the State Attorney that the new Medical Examiner would not be involved in any outside or private practice work—even though these activities were expressly permitted under the State Statutes covering the Medical Examiner system in Florida. The two pathologists consequently had a fairly collegial relationship as both were able to understand that professional differences of opinion should not translate into personal animosity—an understanding that was certainly not universal among members of the forensic pathology community.

The upshot of this situation was that Arthur Lyons was viewed with much more professional congeniality than he frequently experienced when reviewing cases, or examining tissues, at other facilities. He realized, however, that his colleague was being placed in a somewhat precarious position, unbeknownst to himself, in the event this case turned out to be more than the simple drowning that his office had already officially determined. Lyons and Larry had arrived with their usual autopsy dissecting equipment in anticipation of the situations they usually encountered. Typically they were offered little or no help from the office staff, but this time they were pleasantly surprised, and Larry suspicious, when they were offered all the equipment, including photos and x-rays, that they might need to complete their second autopsy examination.

From the start, the assumption was that this was a simple drowning with some minor bruises and scrapes, the result of the body being recovered from the water, having been dragged up the earthen bank of the canal. There were no other areas of significant traumatic injury, as determined from the first autopsy.

The body had been kept under refrigeration since the time of the first autopsy, so there had been little, if any, post-mortem deterioration taking place. The first item of business was to do a careful external examination, at which point multiple linear abrasions, dark red in color, were identified in the upper back involving both shoulder blades and extending downward into the lower back area.

Associated with the abrasions, several areas of bluish discoloration were observed in the back of the neck and mid-back area. These appeared fairly extensive and diffuse, although he and Larry noted that the skin was intact—indicating that this area had not been examined in the first autopsy.

The second exam was being performed in the main autopsy room at the same time two other cases were being dissected. Consequently, there was plenty of company, including Dr.

Stanton and his associate pathologist Don Kacey, both of whom were dividing their attention between their own case and the pair involved in the examination of Henry Freeman.

Dr. Kacey was, actually, the doctor who performed the first autopsy and made the determination that the death was the result of a drowning, adding the circumstances surrounding the death that occurred "while attempting to elude law enforcement."

After Larry had rolled the body on its side, Lyons was in the process of taking a number of photos, documenting both the abrasions and the bruising, when Dr. Stanton called out from across the room and pointedly re-iterated that those injuries "were post-mortem from when they dragged him up the river bank after they pulled him from the water."

Larry turned around slightly and quietly remarked to Lyons, 'I don't think so! There is reddening around the abrasions and that means he was alive, in my book."

Careful examination of the back showed exactly that, and Lyons nodded in agreement, but didn't comment on the assertion just made by the Chief Medical Examiner. He continued to snap close-up photos and completed his sketches of the area.

The next step was to remove the thick thread stitches used to close the head, chest and abdomen after the first autopsy. Then, they proceeded to examine the inside of the chest and abdominal cavities for any internal injuries.

Finding no visible injuries in those areas, they removed the previously dissected organs from the red bio-hazard bag where they had been placed after having been removed during the initial autopsy. Although they were somewhat mixed up, the two went thru it piece by piece with Dr. Lyons dutifully harvesting tissue sections for later microscopic evaluation—recognizing that there was probably limited, if any, histology that had been a part of the first autopsy.

The lung tissues were still very wet with the edema fluid described in the first autopsy and consistent with the findings to be expected from a drowning victim. This wasn't a surprise.

Further examination of the remaining organs including heart, liver, kidneys and brain showed no evidence of any ongoing diseases in this seemingly healthy young man.

The surprises began however, when they began to examine areas that had not been previously dissected during the first autopsy. Dr. Lyons had been alerted to a small area of bleeding in the muscles in the back of the chest by his sharp-eyed forensic tech.

This was far from the first time Larry Hudson had picked up on a subtle and otherwise inconspicuous finding during an autopsy. As the pathologist often joked, "He bailed me out from missing an important finding, that's why we're a team," and this case was no exception.

In order to completely evaluate the injury to the back, they placed the victim face down on the table, allowing access to the spine from the back for a complete examination of the area. From the moment of the initial skin incision into the superficial tissues it was apparent that a significant amount of soft tissue hemorrhage had taken place—the clear result of direct blunt force trauma to the area.

"Geoffrey," Lyons called out. "Take a look at this" pointing to the now-exposed area of extensive bleeding extending from just beneath the skin into the deep muscles actually next to the vertebral column itself.

Drs. Stanton and Kercy both walked over to the autopsy table where Larry was, at this point, beginning to dissect the muscle away from the bone of the spinal column in preparation to sawing the bone and removing the spinal cord itself.

The response of the two was quite different with Dr. Kercy exclaiming, "Wow, I guess I missed this last week," as he looked in obvious surprise at the area Larry was beginning to dissect.

Dr. Stanton, on the other hand was much less committal to say the least. "Arthur, I'll have to look at this a little more closely, but I think it may be just post-mortem settling of blood. You know, livor mortis."

While Larry stared in disbelief, his compatriot was well aware of the situational chess game that had now begun with the Medical Examiner's office. Their position on this death was now being directly challenged. Even the doctor performing the first autopsy had, in effect, acquiesced to the obvious fact that there was unexplained trauma discovered in a victim who had died following some sort of interaction with law-enforcement.

This was a case wherein the official examination by the Medical Examiner had determined the death to be an accidental drowning. But the subsequent examination revealed trauma that the pathologist who performed the first autopsy had spontaneously admitted, in front of Lyons, Larry and the staff of the office, that he had missed!

Needless to say, the atmosphere of mutual professional co-operation began to dissipate fairly quickly following the revelation of the hemorrhage in the back. It essentially disappeared as Larry removed the back of the upper thoracic vertebrae, revealing an acute injury with hemorrhage to the spinal cord itself.

A large amount of blood that flowed out immediately revealed a spinal cord that appeared swollen with blood clinging to the surface but no actual transection. This is a situation where just the force of the object causing the trauma can result in interruption of the ability of the cord to function. Such interruption can often result in a temporary paralysis, a situation known as "spinal shock."

Opening the spinal vertebrae had now become the focal point of activity in the autopsy room, and all the forensic techs and the two pathologists had now joined Larry and Lyons at the dissection table. This was to the obvious discomfort of Dr. Stanton, who began to realize that, with this many witnesses to the event, it was becoming increasingly unlikely that the explanation of 'livor mortis' would be palatable to a group of experienced forensic professionals.

The next step in the process was to gently dissect the now-visible portion of the spinal cord. This process entailed the cutting of the many pairs of nerves emanating from the central cord that would ultimately provide the signals that allowed all parts of the body to function. After disconnecting them, it would allow the cord to be removed from the boney canal where it was housed.

Because the cord was unusually soft, owing to the traumatic forces that had recently been experienced, Arthur Lyons decided to place the entire structure in a formaldehyde fixative that would both preserve and stabilize the tissue prior to the actual cutting.

Since the process of adequate tissue preservation, or fixation, takes at least a couple of days for small pieces of tissue, and even up to a week for a larger structure such as a spinal cord, it would be necessary for Dr. Lyons to take the specimens back to his office to take sections at a later date.

Next, the areas underlying the abrasion injuries on the back were also examined indicating that while there was superficial hemorrhage consistent with a vital injury—meaning that the victim was alive at the time—there was none of the deep hemorrhage there as compared to the injury to the mid-back. Skin biopsies and tissue from the underlying musculature were taken for documentation, but the differences between the scrapes on the shoulder blades and the injury to the spinal cord were obvious to the naked eye!

The explanation for this difference was clear to Dr. Lyons. These represented different and independent injuries. These were a relatively superficial abrasion injury in the shoulder area and a much more serious area of injury to the upper back and spine, which was not associated with any abrasion but more likely the result of a very forceful blow to the area.

While the abrasions could be explained by sliding down an embankment—not from pulling a dead body up out of the water —the injury to the back indicated an assault.

The theory that these were post-mortem changes was clearly ridiculous. In order for the reddish coloration to occur—the so-called 'vital injuries'—these must be the existence of circulation, where blood pressure pushes the blood out of the injured vessels, causing the early manifestation of a bruise.

Once a person is dead, there is no blood pressure!

It had become increasingly apparent that the second autopsy, being performed right there in the Medical Examiner's office surrounded by the doctors and techs that worked there, was unearthing clear findings that were directly contradicting the original findings. It demonstrated that the first autopsy, performed by their pathologist, was seriously inadequate and had likely led to an erroneous diagnosis—maybe even missed a homicide.

There had been a prior agreement between Drs. Stanton and Lyons that the latter would process the tissue samples and provide duplicate microscopic slides to the Medical Examiner, if that became necessary. This was a somewhat unusual situation anyway, particularly since Lyons and his crew had been allowed to come into the facility, and it was assumed that this would be a routine examination, so there should be no issue with their taking any samples for their own analysis.

Things heated up a little however, with the discovery of areas of injury basically contradicting the original diagnosis. Dr. Stanton realized that he would need somehow to explain the discrepancies, and he suddenly panicked at the thought of all the specimens leaving his control.

"Arthur," he said as he walked over to the autopsy table. "I think it might be better if we took custody of the tissues and get the micros done. I can have the lab do duplicates of the slides, and we'll send you a set right away."

"Well Geoffrey," the pathologist replied, "that wasn't exactly what we had planned, since I brought all the containers and cassettes and formalin." But seeing that his colleague was clearly becoming nervous as regards this topic, he said. "But I guess that's not a problem. I know you'll want to review everything too, with all the new evidence!"

"I just think it might be easier all around to do it this way," was the reply. Having no issues with this arrangement, Lyons agreed, and after finishing the dissection, taking all the photos, and making the notes, the visiting pair departed the office and headed back to Orlando.

"That got a little bit weird," Larry turned to Lyons who was pulling the car onto the interstate. "I know the techs were watching real closely and knew exactly what the hell was going on. You can't fool those guys—they've been doing this for years!"

Dr. Lyons gave it a little thought and then responded, "This smells like a real cover-up, Larry. I know that Stanton is going to be under a lot of pressure from here on out to make this an accident somehow."

Enter the State Attorney

Unbeknownst to the group when they were at the autopsy table, as Arthur Lyons would learn later, Dr. Stanton had been in communication with the State Attorney's office during the actual autopsy. He had briefly excused himself from the room, reporting the results of the on-going examination, and requesting guidance as to how he should proceed.

So much for the 'independent' Medical Examiner!

It was apparent to everyone in that autopsy room that the initial determination of a simple drowning after a police encounter was no longer a tenable diagnosis. But the subsequent actions of the chief pathologist—officially in charge of determining the cause and manner of death for the State—from the moment he realized that the second autopsy had uncovered new injuries led Dr. Lyons to view the situation with a considerable degree of skepticism.

Technically, the Medical Examiner's office was under no legal obligation under the governing State Statutes to accept or even consider the results of an independent investigation, in this case the second autopsy performed on Henry Freeman.

If Dr. Stanton chose to do so, he could proceed as if those results simply didn't exist, leaving no real avenue to bring Lyons' findings to light as far as the official investigation and determinations were concerned. It was particularly significant that he'd had direct communication with the State well in advance of even the completion of the dissection stage of the autopsy, let alone what the ultimate findings would be after review and looking at the microscopic slides.

Injury to the spinal cord as evidenced by the examination of the back can result in an interruption of the motor and sensory neural pathways connecting the brain to other parts of the body. It causes either temporary or permanent injury, depending on severity, and interfere with a person's ability to function properly, such as in the case of an experienced swimmer being unable to swim!

Although there were some superficial abrasions on the shoulder blades that might have resulted from contact with the ground at some point, the area of spine injury was not associated with any externally visible injury, and the bruising in the skin was deep. This combined with the intensity of the trauma compared to any other area of the body suggested that a blunt force applied to the area by compression—such as a knee-drop to the middle of the back—was a more likely than not the explanation for the injury pattern observed in the body of Mr. Freeman.

After Stanton had blown-off the explanation provided to him refuting possible post-mortem artifact—livor mortis, or the settling of blood after death—Arthur Lyons had pretty much dismissed the idea of getting an objective response on the newly discovered evidence from him. But he was pleasantly surprised by the reaction of his associate Medical Examiner.

After they had opened the cord and observed the hemorrhaging, Dr. Ron Kercey had come over to the table and remarked, "That sure is a lot of hemorrhage. I am really surprised. What could he have hit that hard?" He clearly indicated that he did not think these were the result of anything happening after Freeman was already dead, and he had actually done the first autopsy!

It appeared to Lyons that the story given by law enforcement didn't comport at all with the degree of trauma and the distribution of injuries that they had determined to be present. So he decided to do some independent investigation himself, and after leaving the office and hurriedly contacting Freeman's sister, he made arrangements to visit the scene of the incident while he and Larry were still in town.

It seemed to take forever for the pair to find their way through a virtual maze of back streets before ending up on a dead end next to a deep irrigation canal with grass-lined banks and a rapidly flowing stream of water. A row of modest middle-income residences probably built in the '60's lined the street with well-kept lawns and front porches, on which a number of the predominately African-American residents were sitting in the late afternoon.

As they pulled up in front of the last house before the canal, they were greeted by a pleasant middle-aged Black woman introducing herself as Jerieka Sanders, who indicated that she was delighted to see them.

"I was hoping you would have a chance to look at where this happened," she said, pointing to the canal. "I have so many questions I hoped you could answer."

Larry was getting out of the car and looked at the deep canal. "I sure as hell hope the Sheriff's guys don't know we're out here! I don't feel like a swim this afternoon," he said.

"Not to worry" Lyons responded in a less than convincing tone. "I don't think they got the word yet."

Lyons turned to Jerieka and began to fill her in on the findings of that day's exam. "Well, they didn't examine the back or the spinal cord before, and we found that there was a lot of trauma—probably enough to have incapacitated him while he was in the water. It doesn't look like it was from falling into the canal."

"How did that happen?" was the next question.

"Looks like he was hit in the back—maybe like a "knee-drop" —sometime before he went into the canal," Lyons responded, "Do we know if anybody saw what actually happened?"

Jerieka Sanders went on to explain that she hadn't actually seen the incident herself as she was inside the house, but several of the neighbors had witnessed the police drag her brother from the car, knock him to the ground and jump on top of him. Then they dragged him back into the bushes and the next she knew they were pulling him from the canal.

While the two were talking, Larry had wandered over across the street. He was talking to two somewhat elderly gentlemen who were sitting on the porch, pointing out toward the canal and gesturing rather animatedly as Lyons and Jerieka approached to find out what was going on.

Apparently, at least one of them had been on the porch the night of the incident and witnessed the entire event from the time Freeman stopped his car until the police dragged him back into the bushes, where they lost sight of him.

"Doc," Larry informed the pathologist. "These guys actually saw the whole thing and are telling me that our guy got beaten up pretty bad before he even got to the water. Doesn't look like an accident to me!"

Jerieka quickly introduced Arthur Lyons to the three men standing on the front porch talking to Larry, who were demonstrably a little nervous when this official-looking white man approached. At first, they didn't show the same degree of comfort that they had a few moments before while conversing with Larry.

After the introduction, the three became much more talkative, explaining the details of the incident.

"I told that reporter before that they pulled Henry out of the car by the arms and kicked and jumped on him over and over. It was awful!" said a middle-aged man, who identified himself as William Deveraux. He walked into his house for a moment only to reappear with his cell phone in hand.

Going on the screen for a few seconds, Deveraux turned the screen so Lyons could see it. "Here take a look at this," he said, and began to show a somewhat darkened, grainy video showing a sea of flashing lights and headlights from a plethora of police cruisers. In the middle of the melee, the image of a figure on the ground surrounded by a number of uniformed officers, some of whom were kicking and "kneeing" him. Moments later, the video showed the man on the ground being picked up by the arms and carried back into the bushes—with his heels dragging behind him, showing no movement at all.

Dr. Lyons and Larry stared at each other in obvious disbelief that there was an actual video of the beating that totally contradicted the official account of the incident.

"Well, I tried to talk to the reporter guy, but the police told me to 'get my Black ass back to my house,'" Mr. Deveraux continued. "I was too scared to tell anybody what I saw—that canal is real deep you know."

Since the video was on an iPhone, Lyons wanted to perform a simple Air-Drop transfer, to which Mr. Deveraux immediately agreed. In a few seconds, two copies of the incident video existed.

All three of the residents basically told similar stories regarding the incident and what happened in the aftermath.

"Nobody even asked me what I saw," Deveraux offered. "They was just walking around with their hands on their guns, thinking they're going to scare everybody to be quiet. And it pretty much worked. Nobody wanted to end up like our neighbor, you know!"

It was clear that the injury to the spinal cord that was discovered during the second autopsy put the entire case into an entirely new perspective—at least as far as Lyons was concerned—fully aware that his opinion would not be met with great enthusiasm from the powers-that-be in the County and State Attorney's office.

If, indeed, the injury had occurred somehow as Freeman slide down the bank of the canal, Lyons had concluded, the most severe trauma would be to the skin and soft tissues. It would have created an obvious area of bruising since the force would be generated from the outside inward. There were only surface abrasions—scrapes—but no contusions—bruising—evident on the skin or underlying soft tissues.

The obvious explanation for these findings would be a force such as a large man coming down on the back with his knee, leaving no external sign of trauma but causing severe injury to the underlying structures, in this case the vertebrae and spinal cord. This fitted neatly into a scenario wherein the victim was impaired, affecting his ability to swim, and then thrown into the canal.

After about an hour at the scene of the death, Larry and Dr. Lyons headed back to Orlando. They had taken multiple pictures of the area, as well as obtaining the copy of the critical video from Mr. Deveraux. Although Larry was a little nervous until they hit the Orange County line, both agreed that this was one of the most eventful days they had seen for a long while.

As part of their original agreement, Lyons was to provide duplicate slides, or recuts, of the samples he processed for examination under the microscope, which included the tissues of the back and the spinal cord.

The Medical Examiner had arranged for him to examine the slides from the first autopsy prior to their performing the second exam, but obviously these had not included the areas of injury that Lyons subsequently discovered. Nonetheless, after examining the slides, he did request a set of recuts in order to have them to refer to in the future.

During his review, Lyons realized that Dr. Stanton was constantly looking over his shoulder and giving 'helpful suggestions' regarding what the slides showed—suggestions that he didn't need or appreciate, given his extensive experience in the field. It was pretty obvious that Stanton was less than comfortable with the situation—to say the least!

The intent however was very obvious, to simply steer Lyons in the direction of accepting what at that point seemed to be a straightforward case of a man running from the police and drowning in an attempt to escape.

This was from his perspective an open-and-shut case from the start. Consequently, the surprise findings would need to be somehow explained away in order not to usurp the original diagnostic findings and create a potentially problematic situation should it point to any inappropriate actions by the police. This was a situation that could prove very precarious for Stanton's future as the District Medical Examiner.

When the tissue from the second autopsy had been processed and the analysis made, it showed large areas of blood infiltrating between muscle fibers and nerve fibers in the spinal cord. This indicated that the injuries occurred while blood was circulating. It confirmed victim was alive.

Bleeding into the skin, muscle, or any other organs or areas of the body require blood pressure so that blood is actually pumped into the injured area, then coming out of small blood vessels that have been disrupted by the traumatic forces. The presence of blood pressure obviously means the person was alive at the time.

In the case of post-mortem 'injury' or the settling of blood designated livor-mortis, there is no active perfusion of the blood into the tissues, since there is no blood pressure. This distinction is usually clear to the naked eye, but in the performance of a complete forensic autopsy, the sampling of questionable areas to later examine under the microscope will clear up any potential questions. This is precisely how Arthur Lyons handled this situation!

The finding of blood outside the blood vessels clearly refuted the contention by the Medical Examiner that the injuries were the result of handling the body after death. This finding supported Lyons' opinion, but it was not, as it turned out, convincing to Dr. Stanton, who doggedly continued to insist he was right, refusing to entertain any other explanations. Most importantly he would not change the official determination from accidental death!

The Cover Up

Arthur Lyons was well-aware of the political forces that all too often become a factor in these high-profile cases. He knew how the Medical Examiner can be subject to potential compromise in making the determination that can easily alter the course of an investigation.

That determination by the Medical Examiner is not only the cause of death, but also the "manner"—whether it's a homicide, an accident, a suicide, or a natural death. The ruling can be a critical factor in any death investigation because if the case is a homicide, a full investigation is launched. Whereas, there is little further action taken if the death is one of the other possibilities.

By categorizing this death as an "accident," the Medical Examiner had given the police a free pass so far as conducting any further inquiry into the event. This precluded the possibility that any legal action would ever be taken against the officers involved.

Kevin Butler was the attorney that Jerieka Sanders, the sister of Henry Freeman, ultimately had hired to look into the circumstances and determine if there was any legal action that she might take in order to hold someone responsible for his death. She initially was reluctant to make waves, fearing for her own well-being as well as for Henry's three minor children whom she was helping raise along with her brother. She immediately changed her mind after hearing from Dr. Lyons the results of his second autopsy.

It was not only the previously undiscovered trauma that caused concern, but it had become apparent almost immediately that the case was going to be called an accidental drowning and quickly swept under the rug. This was to avoid any hint of potential liability on the part of law enforcement in the death.

"Dr. Lyons," the initial phone conversation began. "As you may be aware, I represent the family of Henry Freeman, and we're looking at a wrongful death case. Obviously, your findings are the lynchpin of our argument that this wasn't an accident," as Kevin Butler continued, "so I would like to discuss this further at your convenience."

Although he had had several interactions with Jerieka, the phone call was Lyons' first actual contact with the attorney.

"I'd be happy to work with you, and hopefully we can bring some of the nonsense going on into the light of day," the pathologist replied. He silently wondered if the lawyer had any inkling of how complicated this endeavor was going to be.

"Kevin," Lyons continued, "I'm sure you're aware that I have spoken extensively with the folks at the Medical Examiner's office. They are digging in on this accident theory, and Geoffrey

Stanton is leading the resistance. I think we're in for a long struggle!"

Kevin Butler had practiced law for over twenty years, mostly as a Plaintiff's attorney representing accident victims and patients injured by medical malpractice. He had seldom been involved with situations involving the police, the Medical Examiner, or a governmental bureaucracy seeking to mitigate any damages through whatever means necessary.

Arthur Lyons, on the other hand, had learned through many encounters with this establishment, both in his previous role as a Medical Examiner working in the governmental system, and later in private practice. Where most of his encounters placed him in a position generally viewed by the State as being on the other side, despite the many cases where his objectivity was patently obvious to the most casual observer—that for the most part there was more interest from the government in defending their particular position, regardless of the facts!

"I'm confident we can make some headway in this, with your help," the attorney responded.

"Hell, you don't know what you're getting into," Larry shouted across room from where he was standing. He was in the middle of removing the gut from an autopsy they were performing and privy to the call as Lyons had put his iPhone on speaker.

"Sorry Kevin," Lyons responded. "That's Larry, my forensic tech, who has seen way too many of these types of cases and is always suspicious."

"No problem Doc. He's probably right. I know we're going to get a lot of resistance, but it'll be worth it if we can prove what actually happened."

"Bullshit!" was Larry's partly inaudible response as he walked across the room with a pan full of intestine to the sink where he would continue the dissection.

"Well, that's my man Larry," Lyons laughed as he ended the call.

From the outset, it had become increasingly clear that the authorities, including the Medical Examiner's office, were not at all interested in considering any of the injuries discovered during the second autopsy—at least officially. That position was supported unflinchingly by law enforcement, the County and the State Attorney.

For his part, Arthur Lyons was certainly no stranger to dealing with the political forces that were almost always in play in any high-profile case—particularly if law enforcement or even one of the politicos themselves were involved.

He recalled one case in particular that happened early in his career when, while acting in the capacity of a forensic pathologist working with the local elected Coroner in a county outside Atlanta, he had been called to the scene of a shooting in a dingy motel room on the north side of the city.

The job he had taken soon after he had finished his residency training and passed the board exams to be officially qualified as a forensic pathologist entailed being Medical Examiner in two of the counties ringing Atlanta. One was where a modern system of forensic death investigation had been established, and the doctor was in charge of medically determining the cause and manner of death in any case that was traumatic, suspicious or otherwise might have medicolegal ramifications.

Additionally, it turned out, the County next door was operating under the antiquated Coroner's system. In that country, a citizen, regardless of any particular qualifications, would be elected as the 'Coroner' and put in charge of death investigations. It sought the services of a physician to perform autopsies.

These elected Coroners were often, in the best case, funeral directors or ambulance attendants—having at least some medical knowledge. But they usually were untrained, and in at least one instance in a jurisdiction to the north, it was a gas station attendant!

These elected Coroners usually had minimal if any medical knowledge. They would often, particularly in more urban jurisdictions, employ a forensic pathologist to conduct autopsies and other medical examinations for them in order to establish the cause and manner of death in the cases in which they were involved.

After Dr. Lyons accepted the Medical Examiner job, the opportunity arose to provide forensic pathology services to the Coroner in the adjacent County. This allowed him to expand his practice as well as supplement his income, recognizing that there was a severe flaw in the system. The medical doctor determined the cause of death, while the medically-untrained Coroner would decide the manner of death, whether it was homicide, suicide, accident or natural causes.

Following a telephone call from the County Coroner, it was late afternoon, several months into the job, when after fighting traffic on the infamous I-285 for about 45 minutes, the pathologist arrived at a small 10-room motel. He was greeted by at least twenty police cars with their red lights flashing, filling the parking lot.

"You can't come in here," one burley officer shouted as Lyons pulled into the motel entrance. "Turn the hell around!"

"I'm the Medical Examiner," he called back as he rolled down the window. "The Coroner said we had a scene here."

"Sorry Doc, didn't recognize you," the officer replied apologetically.

"Yeah, I've only been here a month or so, and we've not had a lot of homicides—that's good I guess," Lyons continued.

The doctor had actually only been to one scene prior to this one, and that was a multi-fatality automobile accident. While they had had four homicides, the others died after being transported to hospital, consequently, it was the highway-patrol officers and not sheriff's people at the scene of that incident.

Armed with a set of surgical gloves and his camera, Dr. Lyons entered the motel room and immediately observed the body of a young woman. She appeared to be in her late twenties, lying on the floor face-down with a small amount of blood pooling in the carpet next to her head.

Three detectives were in the room as well, and he recognized two of them as attendees at several of the autopsies of homicide cases he had recently examined.

"Hi Doc, glad you found your way clear out here," said an individual appearing to the lead detective on the case and introducing himself as Derrick Stone. "Looks like she shot herself," he said pointing to the .38 caliber handgun resting in her left hand.

Initial examination of the body of any victim at the apparent scene of the incident is important, but, as Dr. Lyons knew well it was meant to be only a preliminary assessment. Proper management of the evidence entailed moving the deceased in such a way as to minimize any alteration of the wounds or clothing and preventing loss of any "trace" evidence such as hair, fibers, and blood or fluid coming from someone other than the victim.

It was particularly important not to move the body unnecessarily or disturb the clothing, and the protocol was to carefully transfer the deceased to a clean sheet which would be then placed in a plastic shroud. This tactic optimized the potential to recover any items that might fall from the body during the transfer.

"Did you move her at all?" Lyons asked, turning to the detective who now had walked back across the room. There he was talking with a rather large man wearing only blue jeans and standing near the bathroom door of the motel room.

"Yeah Doc, we needed to see where the blood was coming from, so we moved her a little bit, but didn't roll her over. The gun is there in her hand just like it was when we got here."

Looking around the room, it was noted that there were at least five uniformed officers plus the three detectives in this relatively cozy motel room. This was way too many people for proper scene management but a situation that was all too frequent, particularly if the victim was a young, partially clad woman. Everyone wanted to have a look!

The female victim was noted to have her blouse open and her underwear partially removed, immediately suggesting to Lyons that this was not a run-of-the-mill suicide, recalling his conversation with the lead detective at the scene:

"Doc, this guy was with her and says she just went crazy. She grabbed the gun and shot herself while he was trying to take it away from her—to keep her from injuring herself," Detective Stone continued, pointing to the bare-chested, rather obese white man standing next to the sink. "Sounds reasonable, but I'm not buying it completely 'til we get the autopsy done."

There was a lot of blood surrounding the face, mostly dried. It wasn't until the body was brought back to the morgue—an autopsy room recently established by the County to provide a place to perform Coroner's autopsies—and the blood removed, that in addition to the gunshot wound to the right temple area, a second wound was found in the middle of the left cheek!

"Look at this," Lyons turned to Stone who had attended the autopsy as a routine follow-up of an apparent suicide. "We've got two gunshots—sort of shoots the hell out of the suicide theory!"

It was now becoming more critical to ascertain the range and trajectory of both wounds, documenting the damage done. He had to determine what vital structures were compromised by the trauma of the bullet striking them.

"Doc, how close was the gun to her?" Stone had asked, now looking more than a little confused.

The wound on the cheek had a small amount of "stippling"—small punctate burns caused by hot gunpowder that comes from the barrel as the bullet exits. This indicated that the range of fire was about one to two feet, but not much closer due to the absence of gunpowder which is usually deposited on the skin if the gun is closer than about ten inches.

The wound to the right temple area of the skull showed no stippling, but did show black soot material in the tissues immediately below the hole in the skin. This indicated that the barrel of the gun was in contact with the skin, and all the burning and unburned soot was forced into the wound itself—a so-called "press contact" wound.

Upon opening the skull, an examination of the brain showed that the wound of the temple had penetrated the brain, causing extensive destruction of the areas involved in motor function. The wound of the cheek had transected the brainstem—causing immediate interruption of all motor and sensory nerves to the entire body.

He carefully removed the brain that was now partially pulpified due to the force of the bullet passing through.

Lyons explained to Detective Stone, "The bullet itself does damage but the force generated by the speed of the projectile is more widespread and tears up a lot more tissue than the bullet itself. That's why we have so much damage!"

"Either of these injuries would have resulted in immediate incapacitation, with no ability to perform any type of activity" Lyons continued. "Therefore, it's clear that after the first wound, whichever it was, she couldn't have inflicted the second one! This is no suicide!"

"Well Doc," Stone turned to Lyons as he was walking out, saying he'd seen enough. "This is the worst suicide I've ever seen. We're going to arrest that jackass she was with for murder!" Although the cause of death was clearly the result of the two gunshot wounds, it was important for the pathologist to perform a complete autopsy. This was in order to evaluate any other processes going on that might ultimately affect the final determination as to the cause and manner of death, but also to shed light on other potential questions that might arise.

Examination of the arms showed only a few areas of reddish discoloration on the outside of the right wrist but upon making an incision into the area, Lyons was able to demonstrate hemorrhage into the soft tissues. It was a clear indication of blunt force, in this case, probably someone forcibly grabbing the wrist of the young victim.

After getting Stone on the phone, Lyons explained, "You left too early, we found some other injuries, and it looks like somebody grabbed her wrist pretty hard!"

Stone responded to say he wasn't surprised and for Lyons to take good pictures, as he was on his way to make an arrest.

Upon completion of the autopsy, the pathologist went back to his office, which for the time-being, was in a small room adjacent the morgue facility. He began to translate his notes into a Dictaphone that would ultimately be transcribed into a report. Additionally, he filled out the paperwork to send over to the Coroner, who, under the present system, would actually fill out the death certificate. This death certificate included not only the cause of death, but whether it would be ruled a suicide or a homicide!

While the Coroner technically had the final say in the issuing of these death certificates, it would be unusual for the opinion of the forensic pathologist to be overridden. This certainly didn't seem to be an instance where this type of action would be anticipated—it was a clear-cut multiple gunshot wound homicide!

While there were many Coroners in the State of Georgia that were little qualified from either the medical or legal perspective, Lyons had been pleasantly surprised when he accepted the position as Coroner's pathologist. He found that the office was jointly shared by a group of attorneys who divided up the responsibilities among the four lawyers.

At least, he thought, these guys understood the legal side, and he'd be able to work with them effectively. For the most part, this turned out to be true, with Lyons submitting the findings of the autopsy with recommendations as to the Manner of Death, and the Coroner signing the death certificate in accord with his opinions.

The positions had opened up in both counties in January and by early Spring everything had been running smoothly—up until the events surrounding the death in the motel room. The cases for the Coroner were running about fifty percent less that those he performed as Medical Examiner. This was primarily because of budgetary constraints imposed by the Coroner, as an elected official looking forward to the next election, and trying to do death investigation on the cheap. He often failed to order autopsies in cases that in most jurisdictions would be considered appropriate, if not essential for an accurate determination to be made.

Lyons had turned in the information on the motel death in early April, and he basically forgot about the case. He assumed that it would be finalized by the Coroner's office within a few days as had been the case in most all of the cases he had handled since he'd been there doing autopsies.

Consequently, he was very surprised, to say the least, when he received a call from Detective Stone. The detective was inquiring about the case and asking why it hadn't been signed out.

"Doc," he remembered being asked. "What are you waiting on?" he asked somewhat impatiently. "I thought this was a slam-dunk but the Coroner still hasn't made the call."

"I'm not sure what's the problem," the pathologist responded. "I'll give them a call to see what is the hang-up."

After hanging up the phone with Stone, Lyons immediately called the Coroner's office and spoke with the lawyers' secretary. She could only tell him that the case was under review and had no further information. This immediately aroused a certain amount of concern for even a relatively neophyte forensic pathologist as to what else was going on here!

Arthur went back to his office and began to review the report and pictures again, wondering if there were any possible issues that he'd missed. He finally decided to send the case to two of his prior mentors—nationally known pathologists with whom he had trained—to get their opinions and possible advice as to how to proceed. He also wanted either to confirm or modify his diagnosis in this case.

Despite his inexperience and political naivete, there was an immediate recognition that everything may not be kosher in this situation. He knew it'd be a good idea to get some outside advice

—a mindset that would prove to be very beneficial both in this case and in his future practice.

Finally getting a return call from David Mahaffey, one of the members of the law firm functioning as Coroner, Dr. Lyons immediately requested information about the status of the case of the death in the motel room.

He recalled asking, "David, what's the hold-up? I'm getting a lot of questions from law enforcement."

The Coroner went on to explain that they were reviewing the case and hadn't made a final determination. They had received some outside opinions that this might be a suicide.

As Lyons recalled, this statement was a lightning bolt, jarring him into the realization that these guys were not really interested in his diagnosis. For some reason, they were overriding him and calling this a suicide.

It turned out that his gut-feeling was correct. The Coroner officially determined that the death was indeed a suicide, and that she inflicted both wounds herself. Apparently, they had enlisted the expertise of a former Medical Examiner from an adjoining state who had been forced to retire a few years before because of improprieties in his office. He had been doing some part-time work for them before Dr. Lyons took the job.

The opinion rendered was that the victim most-likely discharged the gun while holding it first against her temple, and then as she was falling, pulled the trigger again with the gun now away from her head, the second wound entered the left cheek.

At a press conference subsequently called by the Coroner, the consultant pathologist suggested that Dr. Lyons, because of his inexperience, had jumped the gun in calling this a homicide. He said this probably was because Dr. Lyons had never seen a suicide in which the weapon had been discharged twice, and that he as a more experienced pathologist, had seen several previous cases where two gunshots had been self-inflicted.

The press conference had been rather hastily called, and the case explained to the cameras by the consulting pathologist. Dr. Lyons not only was not invited, but only found out about it shortly after it was over when another detective from the county called him.

"Doc, you're not going to believe this. The Coroner just gave a news conference, and they are calling our motel case a suicide!"

After having become aware of the very questionable politics in this particular County, Dr. Lyons was not shocked anymore by anything that might come out of the Coroner's office. He responded, "I guess these guys aren't interested in the facts, so there must be more to this case than meets the eye!" He added, "We won't be prosecuting this as a homicide, that's for sure."

For a number of months, not much information had been forthcoming regarding that particular case. None of the lawyers had given any kind of explanation as to their decision, and Lyons was pretty much in the dark until he opened a correspondence from the Office of the Coroner containing a notice of a hearing on a case in Alabama.

At first, he couldn't figure out why he was receiving the document, since it was a criminal drug-trafficking issue. It clearly didn't involve any case he was involved in. Then, he noticed the name of the defendant on the case and remembered where he'd heard it before—it was the same guy who was the shooter in the motel room!

It took the pathologist a few minutes to put two-and-two together, but he soon realized that someone had sent him this notice, either mistakenly or intentionally, because it indicated that the lawyers who were the Coroners in Georgia were defense lawyers in Alabama. In fact, they were the defense lawyers for the man whom Lyons was convinced had committed murder in that motel room—the shooting that these same Coroners had ruled a suicide.

To add insult to injury, Lyons later found out that the shooter-drug trafficker was the son-in-law of one of the senior judges in the County criminal court, and he was good buddies with all the lawyers in the Coroner's Office.

The realization then began to set in that the Medical Examiner's findings and opinions were only of interest when they coincided with the needs of the politicos in any particular situation. As long as it was an automobile accident, a heart-attack victim, or a shooting in the inner-city community, his opinion was valued. But if a high-profile case happened, involving any part of the political hierarchy, he might as well be pissing in the wind if he thought his opinion had any bearing on the ultimate disposition of the case.

It was a difficult lesson to learn for a young Medical Examiner, but it would hone his political instincts for problems encountered down the road. He would explain to Kevin Butler that they could expect nothing but resistance in trying to figure out how Henry Freeman ended up in that canal.

For starters, Chief Medical Examiner Geoffrey Stanton had essentially refused to accept the reality of the injuries that Arthur Lyons had uncovered during the second autopsy. The one that was performed while he was actually physically in the morgue, watching the dissection with his own eyes.

He obviously needed to keep his job and not buck the system as he had done before only to be rewarded by being fired!

Even though associate Medical Examiner Dr. Donald Kacey had essentially agreed with the interpretation Lyons had made at the time, it would turn out that he modified his conclusions following a visit from the State Attorney. In that visit he was apparently counseled to be less forthcoming in the future with any cases involving the office, placing political consideration above scientific forensic analysis. That is, if he wanted to maintain his current employment status!

The theory espoused by Dr. Stanton basically attributed the injuries on the back to post-mortem artifact. He said these injuries resulted from the body being dragged out of the canal after he was recovered from the water—a time when Freeman was obviously deceased.

Tissue samples of the areas of hemorrhage were taken during the re-examination, and after review under the microscope, there was no question that these were not post-mortem changes.

Diffuse areas of bleeding into the tissues and outside the blood vessels were obvious to any competent forensic pathologist!

The State Attorney had already denounced the findings of the second autopsy even before all the tissue slides had been evaluated. This clearly indicated that he wasn't going to change his opinion based upon a bunch of 'facts' and had no interest in even finding out what anyone had discovered outside of his own Medical Examiner.

It was becoming increasingly obvious that there was going to be no investigation, let alone prosecution, of any of the individuals involved in this case. The only entity that could initiate such an investigation was the State Attorney, and this was clearly a dead-end!

Commencing Civil Litigation

Armed with the latest microscopic findings from the second autopsy, Arthur Lyons approached the attorney representing the Freeman family. He wanted to discuss the results and determine what further steps could be taken in view of the intransigent position of the County officials and the State Attorney himself.

"Kevin," Lyons volunteered after the attorney called returning his cell-phone text. "This is a textbook case of covering up an in-custody death where there was at least negligence—if not outright homicide."

"Well, where do we go from here?" the attorney responded. "I think we have enough to go ahead with a civil suit if you're on board with it."

"I'm definitely on board," the pathologist responded, "but I think we've got a long road ahead of us."

There was a distinct difference between the pursuit of a criminal case and bringing a civil lawsuit against any or all of the parties involved. In this case it would be considered negligent actions that resulted in a 'wrongful' death, but not actually a homicide—a designation that is not a part of Civil litigation.

While a Criminal conviction required that the case be proven beyond reasonable doubt, in a Civil case, the plaintiff bringing the lawsuit only had to show that the negligent actions more likely than not led to the death.

And while it was hard for either of them to fathom that the police didn't act intentionally, it was the only avenue open to bring the situation into the courtroom, given the outright refusal of the State to pursue the case further.

One of the occupational hazards for a doctor practicing forensic medicine either within a Coroner/Medical Examiner's office or performing forensic exams on living patients—such as assault or abuse situations where it may be necessary to both document traumatic injuries as well as collect evidentiary materials that can be later potentially utilized in the courtroom—is the view that the professional scientist is on the side of the State by virtue of the fact that they are usually employed by a State or County agency.

Consequently, in the prosecution of these type of cases, the doctor or healthcare provider—often nurses in the case of sexual assault exams—is expected to support the Prosecutor's side when evaluating, and more importantly, when testifying in the legal proceedings.

Usually this presented no problem in that the Medical Examiner would make a decision as to whether or not a case was a homicide or if the individual died in some other manner—for example suicide or accident, or even a natural death.

If it was determined not to be homicide, there would usually be no further involvement of the State from the standpoint of pursuing a legal case. The findings of the Medical Examiner would seldom be contested.

The one glaring exception to this was the situation which now confronted not only Arthur Lyons, but the Medical Examiner Geoffrey Stanton as well. A potential homicide had been perpetrated by someone acting in the official capacity of the State, in this case the police themselves!

Because he'd been through this scenario before, Lyons was acutely aware of all the potential problems that could arise. The Medical Examiner making the call in these types of situations could face the prospect of losing their job if they were to vociferously challenge the law enforcement community and determine a police-related death as a homicide.

In many jurisdictions around the country, including Florida, the hiring of a pathologist for the Medical Examiner's position was made by a committee. This committee consisted of members of the State Attorney's office, representatives from all the police and Sheriff's departments in the jurisdiction—usually at least five or six individuals—an attorney from the Public Defender's office, a funeral director, a representative of County government, and a member of the civilian community, usually designated by someone in the county administration.

Because these committees were heavily weighted in favor of the State or City agencies, getting on the wrong-side of any of those people could create difficulties for the doctor, not only during contract renewal time, but even while being hired in the first place. Rumors often were circulated regarding the ability of a candidate to be able to cooperate and get warm and fuzzy with law enforcement, as Arthur Lyons was once advised to do by a member of the selection committee for a job he was applying for! This process was obviously not the ideal arrangement for a forensic scientist. It is his job to gather and evaluate the facts related to a death, including performing autopsies that documented injuries and disease processes, as well as collecting pertinent data that could be used as evidence in legal proceedings or findings that were helpful in determining why a person died.

Although this situation existed in many jurisdictions, many of his colleagues seemed disbelieving when Lyons would bring up the issue during lectures or at professional meetings. This was an indication that they had not yet encountered such a high-profile case where these forces might be brought to bear.

"Kevin," Lyons continued. "We have all the injuries documented in the pictures and now we have the micros that prove our contention that he wasn't able to swim properly because of the injuries. I'd like to send our autopsy findings to someone out of state to take a look."

"Sounds like a great idea," the attorney responded. "Have anyone in mind?"

"I do," Lyons responded. "He's a former chief Medical Examiner in New York who has had a lot of experience in dealing with controversial cases, particularly with police-custody deaths, and I've known him for a number of years. We often get together at one of the forensic meetings. I think he'll give us a fair review and will be available later to testify if he agrees with us."

Arthur Lyons knew one thing for sure. His chosen consultant would give a fair and accurate assessment of the case and not simply tell them what they wanted to hear. He found this was a concept that apparently eludes many forensic experts that contract as independent consultants to analyze and render opinions regarding both forensic medicine and forensic science in general.

There is a pervasive trend to assume that the attorneys want 'experts' that basically support their theories of a particular case. The consultants often act accordingly, striving to maintain an ongoing relationship with that particular individual, looking forward to more consulting business in the future.

Arthur Lyons had been through this drill before and had discovered that actually what the attorney usually wanted was an accurate evaluation of the facts of the case. The attorney did not want to be told what the expert thought he or she wanted to hear.

"I've often said that the attorney wants to know the truth, and then will decide whether or not he will use it in his case!" Lyons told Butler.

"You're right, Arthur," he responded. "But usually we'll use it to decide whether to go ahead with the case, or cut our losses and plead guilty."

Lyons chuckled to himself, thinking that there was at least a little glimmer of hope that the justice system might actually be functional.

The prospect of challenging the findings of an official investigation by the institutions generally perceived by the public as being authoritarian was somewhat of a daunting task under the best of circumstances. But when combined with accusations against law-enforcement, the situation was made even more precarious.

These types of cases were seldom settled before trial, there was often the spectrum of citizens serving as jurors. The jurors would sit in judgement of the same officers with whom they often had at least some contact in the course of their everyday activities—since most often these cases ended up being tried in the local communities—and there was a deep-lingering concern that since the police would know the identity of the jurors, possible retaliation could occur if they ruled against them.

In some circumstances, particularly when there was a great deal of publicity around a case, the attorneys would request a change of venue in order to move the case to somewhere out of the area. This was due with the hope of finding jurors who would be less vulnerable to possible outside influences—but that was also somewhat rare since the judges, also elected officials, didn't want to potentially alienate their constituent voters by giving the impression that they didn't trust them to make an unbiased and informed decision.

This was the situation confronting Kevin Butler and Arthur Lyons as they approached the prospect of filing a civil lawsuit alleging the wrongful death of Henry Freeman at the hands of the police.

Although Dr. Lyons and the other professionals to whom he had referred the case for consultation had been in complete agreement with his analysis, there was the remaining obstacle of the official designation of an accidental death by the Medical Examiner. There also was the implicit assumption that would be made by many of the average citizenry serving on the jury, that the official account was correct, and the outsiders, particularly the experts, were simply trying to exploit the system for monetary gain.

Unfortunately for the ultimate long-term benefits that may be gained from the introduction of unbiased science into the legal system, the attorneys—most often the prosecutors from the State

Attorney's office—were the first on-board to critique the opinions of outside experts. Outside experts were defined as anybody who didn't work directly for the State and were considered unreliable, 'hired guns' whose opinions could not possibly be reliable.

The fact that the scientists on the State's payroll were actually more subject to potential bias—however subtle—due to the necessity of keeping their jobs, was often overlooked.

The job of the prosecutor had become attempting to discredit these experts in order to win their case, but not to actually arrive at the truth. This goal was not in concert with their constitutional mandates, but did, if successful, enhance their chances of winning, regardless of whether or not justice was served!

"Larry, it looks like we've got another good case here," the pathologist turned to his reliably consistent tech. "The lawyer wants to go ahead with the lawsuit."

"Is this our Black mermaid case?" Larry responded somewhat derisively. He was helping to remove the ruptured spleen of a seventeen-year-old boy who had been found in his apartment by his girlfriend following chemotherapy for a malignant tumor of the testes, now presenting with an abdomen full of blood.

"Those white boys sure as hell don't want to rush into anything, do they?" Larry continued. "I wonder how long this is going to take to get any results? Don't want to go too fast, might even stumble on the truth!" Larry mused as he turned back to the autopsy at hand.

The spleen of this young boy was very enlarged resulting from the chemotherapy, and the victim had fallen in his apartment the day before, causing a trauma that would be incidental to a normal person. It turned out to be enough to rupture the spleen and create a severe hemorrhage into the abdomen, resulting in his death.

The local Medical Examiner's office on the west coast had initially reviewed the case but turned it down when their investigator saw the diagnosis of seminoma in the medical records. Given his rudimentary medical knowledge, he assumed this to be a terminal condition, despite the nearly ninety percent cure rate documented in the medical literature and in actual practice.

Interestingly enough, after Dr. Lyons had reported the results of the private autopsy requested by the family after their request was declined by the Medical Examiner, that same investigator called demanding all the tissue and photos and driving the one hundred and thirty miles to Dr. Lyons office to procure the specimens, threatening him in the process for not reporting the case quickly enough. Go figure!

Responding to Larry's earlier comment, Lyons remarked that, "it wasn't like they wanted to give us anything; it's just that they can't escape a civil suit by sweeping it under the rug like the State can!"

This particular case was somewhat unique from the start, in that it was going to be based upon the factual information generated by the second autopsy with little if any official support from the Medical Examiner, the County or law enforcement. Only the Sheriff was really on the hook for any potential damages —the good old boys liked to stick together!

A number of issues had arisen in the months following Dr. Lyons' involvement in the case that were of concern to him. He was attempting to piece together a scenario that would adequately explain the injuries on the body as well as correlating them with the various accounts of the events. These came both from eyewitnesses and from the seemingly less reliable information from law enforcement, the latter whom had essentially refused to give any more detail than that contained in their official press releases.

The traumatic injury that resulted in at least partial incapacitation of Freeman was never explained by anyone besides Arthur Lyons. He had pretty-well linked it to the kicks and possible knee-drop to the upper back as reported by several bystanders who had witnessed the incident from their front porches.

The lack of significant abrasions on the back indicated that this injury was not from sliding down the canal bank, offered as an explanation by the Medical Examiner's office. It was rather from a direct injurious force being delivered to the back, leaving no marks on the skin surface.

Postulating from a medical standpoint, such trauma could cause a temporary loss of motor function to the body, involving the legs for sure and possibly the arms as well. The pathologist felt that this correlated well with the description of Mr. Freeman being "dragged backwards into the woods" by at least three uniformed officers—and he looked for some corroborating data to back-up that theory.

Drag marks on Mr. Freeman's shoes were evident in photos of the body taken at the scene. This potential evidence would tend to support the theory that he was injured in the vicinity of his vehicle, and subsequently moved while having no control of his legs—hence the "dragging."

Through attorney Kevin Butler, all the clothing, including the shoes, had been requested from the State, and although Lyons had requested to see these items at the time of the second autopsy, they had never been provided.

"Dr. Lyons," Butler began on the phone. "You know we'd asked for the clothes and shoes from the ME's office, but they just finally told me that all those items have been destroyed. Their policy is to only keep them for six weeks, they told me."

"It's not like I haven't seen this bullshit before," was the reply. "I doubt they kept it that long once they figured out how important it might be. Guess they're smarter than we gave them credit for!"

"So are we at a dead-end on this part?" the attorney continued.

"Not really, we've got some decent pictures from the scene showing the marks on the heels of the shoes. We know that they brought the body up the bank from the canal using a gurney and a hoist, so there wasn't any dragging there."

Because Lyons had received a number of photos taken electronically at the scene by the Medical Examiner investigator, he was able to analyze them carefully, including magnifying them on the computer. At that point the drag-marks became clear.

One of the great benefits of using digital photography is the ability to study photos in much more detail than would be possible with the old printed pictures, including magnifying specific areas to reveal previously unnoticed detail.

This was the case with the photos from the Medical Examiner. The videos and photos from law enforcement that he was able to access after several months of negotiations—even though they were clearly public records—were not of the same quality, but usable.

There was no doubt in his mind that the Sheriff's department recordings corresponded with the images on Deveraux's cell phone. These images, to this point, had never seen the light of day except for Lyons and Butler.

On-point though, although these recordings were, in part, the same and recorded on several of the police dashcams, they didn't show as well the specific moment when Freeman was kicked and dragged away.

After receiving the cell images, Lyons had pretty much put them on the back-burner for the time being. He did, however, share the fact of their existence with attorney Butler.

But since no one had ever officially questioned Deveraux or anyone else, the pathologist felt no particular obligation to share that information. Both he and the attorney realized that it could potentially be a valuable piece of information to be presented to a jury—and consequently, discoverable if the attorney decided to use it in the courtroom.

Arthur Lyons had always been moderately amused at the idea of discovery in legal proceedings. It required both sides to essentially provide the opposite party with all the evidentiary information they intended to use at trial.

He always joked that the process simply allowed the attorneys time to come up with alternative 'explanations' for the facts presented by the opposing side and developing 'alternate facts.'

This type of discovery was not uniform for States across the country, with many jurisdictions opting for simply presenting the facts for the first time during trial. It is called "trial by ambush," which in many respects, provided a more balanced presentation of the facts.

In any event, Florida courts permitted discovery, so for this case all of the evidence, including the cell-phone videos would ultimately be revealed to the defendants in the civil lawsuit that was being pursued.

They realized that the documentation from the video coupled with the injuries found by Dr. Lyons would most likely come as a complete surprise. While they were aware of the autopsy findings —having been dutifully informed by Dr. Stanton—the connection between the incident and those findings would present a significant problem for the defendant law enforcement officers.

There was incontrovertible evidence, at least in the minds of both Arthur Lyons and Kevin Butler, that the actions of the police actually represented a deliberate action to injure the victim. In all probability, the police subsequently physically threw him into the canal where he drowned.

They found that it would be difficult to envision a scenario that could be characterized other than a homicide—a deliberate action that resulted in a death. But the practical reality was that since the State was not interested in further prosecution, no charges would ever be filed absent the pressure of public outcry. That seemed highly unlikely in this community where African Americans were still considered by many to be second-class citizens.

Nonetheless, they decided to pursue the legal remedies in the civil court arena with the goal of proving that it was the deliberately negligent actions on the part of law enforcement that led to the death of Henry Freeman.

Perhaps the revelations brought to light in the public forum of a jury trial would prompt some future action in regard to beginning a criminal prosecution of those individuals involved. Perhaps it would arouse the community's attention and in the process create enough public pressure to force the politicians to respond appropriately, and do the right thing. But no one was holding their breath!

The Trial

The case dragged out for almost two full years. Finally, it was brought before a jury in the civil proceedings charging a wrongful death lawsuit against the Sheriff's Department and several of the individual officers involved in the altercations surrounding the arrest of Henry Freeman.

The family and their attorney had filed a lawsuit within a few weeks of learning from Dr. Lyons that the death had not been the result of a drowning, as had been officially reported by the Medical Examiner, and not an accident as was reported on the official death certificate. But the attorneys for the defense had created multiple roadblocks along the way, attempting to delay any actual trial for as long as possible.

Every time a document or piece of evidence would be requested, the Sheriff's lawyers would ask for clarification, provide something other than that requested, claim they couldn't find the items requested, or simply ignore the request. This necessitated going through the sometimes protracted legal proceedings of obtaining a subpoena, whereupon the items would finally appear, but after weeks or often months had passed.

Arthur Lyons was well aware of the strategy behind such moves. Memories of witnesses could become more vague—particularly if members of the law enforcement community had paid a few visits to their neighborhoods in the interim—items of evidence could be misplaced, destroyed or become altered due to improper handling, and community interest and concerns could lessen due to the passage of time.

So it was not an ineffective course to follow if a guilty party strove to decrease the chances of being subjected to adverse outcomes in the event the suit went to trial. A group of citizens would make a determination as to the merits of the case, primarily through the testimony of witnesses and the results of analysis of critical pieces of evidence—things that might not be available if memories faded, witnesses were pressured and evidence disappeared.

In the weeks leading up to the trial, a considerable amount of work would become necessary in order to put all the data they had accumulated into a rational presentation which a jury of twelve average citizens could understand. Members of the jury, for the most part, had little if any knowledge of forensic science, and for many this would be their first experience being on a jury.

The pathological findings from the autopsy would be one of two critical pieces of information that would need to be clearly presented and meticulously explained. A panel of lay-persons generally was not familiar with either forensic science or medicine—always a challenge for a pathologist like Arthur Lyons.

Equally important would be the analysis of the scene with reconstruction of the events leading up to Mr. Freeman ending up in that canal and backing up any suppositions with hard factual evidence.

One of the issues would be whether Freeman was thrown into the canal and if that would be possible since the bank was about ten feet high at the point the body was retrieved.

While he and Dr. Lyons were visiting the scene following the autopsy, Larry had wandered back into the wooded area where the victim had been dragged. He had noticed a point where the bank was much lower and had a straight vertical drop to the water of about five feet. He reported to the doctor that he thought someone could be thrown from there without ever hitting the bank on the way down.

"You know Doc, there weren't any marks on the body where he slid down the bank. This looks like he could have jumped or be tossed into the water from here without hitting anything," Larry had opined.

Judging by the injury to the spinal cord, it was clear that he couldn't have moved very much let alone jumped after that trauma. In addition, there weren't any objects he could have impacted on the way down without leaving some abrasions or bruising.

Additionally, there was the video showing first the officers hitting him after which he was being taken back into the woods with his legs dragging motionless behind him.

All this evidence would need to be presented by the plaintiff—in this case the family through their attorney—with experts, including Arthur Lyons. This was an effort to paint an accurate picture of the incident and, of equal importance, to explain how the actual mechanism of injury and death was determined.

During his career as a Medical Examiner, it was an integral part of the job to present the science to jurors in a way they could readily comprehend, regardless of their individual backgrounds and experience because they usually possessed little direct knowledge of forensic medicine. In doing so, it was necessary to walk a fine line, acting as a teacher while not appearing to be patronizing, lest he run the risk of losing credibility.

In past experience the use of visuals turned out to be a very effective way to convey information to the jury. With pictures they could actually see what the doctor was talking about, and while the images would usually require some explanation, there was a level of credibility attained because the jurors become active participants in the process. They could follow along with the pathologist as he went thru the evidence, even though the actual images might require some explanation. They would be seeing it for themselves!

It was clear that the autopsy findings along with the videos from the scene would be the most significant evidence that would be presented in the plaintiff's case. This was the effort to prove that the death was the result of negligence on the part of the arresting officers.

The problem that confronted both Arthur Lyons and Kevin Butler was that this was a 'negligence' approach. Essentially the Civil litigation was necessitated by the failure of anyone in authority to pursue what would, in any other circumstance, be a clear-cut homicide.

"Kevin," the pathologist had reiterated, "if anyone in the civilian community had done anything remotely resembling throwing somebody into a canal after giving them a beating, this would be screaming out for the death penalty or life without parole at the least."

"You're absolutely right," the attorney responded. "But if the authorities won't do anything, our only recourse is to file a wrongful death in Civil Court," affirming that this was a serious flaw in the justice system.

Over the years Arthur Lyons had encountered this situation more often than he'd like to acknowledge. Being somewhat of a purist as regards the justice system—the lady with the blindfold and all that—he knew well that there was an inherent bias in that system, primarily because of the biases that existed in the minds of the people who were running it.

"Doc, do you think the system just doesn't work?" Larry had asked while he was sitting in on a conference between Lyons and Butler. "It always looks like we get screwed in the process, especially Black folks."

While the general public tended to view the justice system as a neutral arbiter of legal questions in both the criminal and civil arenas, those more intimately acquainted with the situation knew better. Unfortunately, the reach of politics too often extends into this realm, creating situations that may be far removed from the ideals of equal justice for which the system was created.

One of the most common occurrences with which Dr. Lyons and many of his colleagues were familiar was in the way cases were charged based upon how the publicity would affect the image of the office. This was an important factor due to the fact that in virtually all jurisdictions across the country the Prosecutors were elected officials were usually campaigning for re-election every four years.

One of the most effective courses of action for a prosecutor to follow in order to enhance his or her image of a "law and order" lawyer was to over-charge a homicide suspect. This was done sometimes even to the point of asking for the death penalty under circumstances that were questionable as to whether or not the offense warranted such a penalty.

A number of years earlier Lyons had been involved in a situation wherein a twenty-five-year-old woman was found dead, partially decomposed and wrapped in a blanket in her bedroom closet after having been reported missing for several days. The Medical Examiner had ruled the cause of death as a homicide, with the woman's boyfriend the primary person of interest.

Even though there was no definite evidence connecting him with the death, he was subsequently arrested. His arrest was based on the circumstance that the couple had had a heated argument in a crowded bar several days earlier—with many witnesses—and she had not been seen since they left the establishment together.

Because of this, and the high level of media attention that had been generated by the woman's disappearance, the State Attorney decided not only to charge the boyfriend with murder, but also to seek the death penalty in the case.

Arthur Lyons was called in after the fact by the defense to review the case, which the Medical Examiner had ruled strangulation homicide based upon the findings of what he thought was blood in the tissues of the neck. He had presumed that this was the result of compression of the neck by either the hands or a ligature.

The Medical Examiner had not taken any tissues for microscopic examination, but he had retained all of the neck organs, preserved in formaldehyde. Lyons was to subsequently examine and take samples from these preserved organs

Evaluation of the tissue under the microscope indicated that what was thought to be hemorrhage was actually the result of decomposition—not trauma—and that the drugs that were found in her blood were the most-likely cause of death.

The boyfriend had indicated all along that they had been using drugs, and after she collapsed and became unconscious, he had been afraid to call 911 because he thought he probably would be arrested. When she failed to wake up he hid the body and left the apartment, but he was insistent that he never injured her—a scenario that was quite plausible in light of the ultimate interpretation of the findings from the review of the autopsy tissues.

When Dr. Lyons reported his findings during a pre-trial deposition by the State, the Prosecutor was somewhat taken aback. He indicated that he would discount any of Dr Lyons opinions and stick with his Medical Examiner, who didn't even examine the microscopic slides from the tissues and simply declared them to be irrelevant.

The State continued to pursue the death penalty in the case, despite the fact that it was clear that the diagnosis of strangulation was not supported by the facts. The attorneys primarily didn't want to take the political heat for dismissing a case that they had for months touted as showing their tough law-and-order approach to criminality.

Fortunately, for the boyfriend, the jury was able, due in no small part to the presentation of the basic scientific facts by Arthur Lyons, to recognize the fallacy of the State's position and found him not guilty. The result of this verdict engendered unwarranted animosity by the Prosecutor toward Lyons with no recognition that an innocent man had been spared from what potentially could have been an execution.

In a virtually unprecedented action, the State Attorney filed a complaint to the State Board of Licensure asking that Dr. Lyons' license to practice medicine be revoked based upon his alleged false testimony at the trial. For their credit, the board summarily dismissed these accusations out of hand, but not before the pathologist had incurred about ten thousand dollars in legal fees required to defend his case—three times what his entire fee had been for involvement in the case in the first place!

This tactic raised the spectra of a potentially powerful weapon of deterrence against any forensic scientist that dared to challenge the State. This, effectively, could deprive a criminal defendant of his or her Constitutional rights for an effective defense against the charges brought against them!

In the case of Henry Freeman, the exact opposite had occurred. Decisions as to whether or not to charge someone with a crime resulted from the real concern of the State Attorney that the political backlash from charging police officers with homicide would potentially hurt his chances for re-election in this majority White community.

Civil lawsuits, in contradistinction to the Criminal Courts, the plaintiff, and in this case the family of the deceased, are required to prove that more likely than not there was negligence involved in the death. This standard is opposed to the standard of beyond a reasonable doubt required for conviction for a criminal offense.

As part of the presentation by the plaintiff, Arthur Lyons and Reginald Baker, who was an expert in the area of police policies and procedures would be called by the primary experts to provide analyses of the case, along with several of the eyewitnesses from the neighborhood. Although William Deveraux had a video from his phone of the incident, the judge had ruled that it was not admissible due to a chain of custody issue—no one could actually prove that the video was authentic, at least in the opinion of the judge—so Deveraux only could testify verbally as to what he witnessed that night.

The jury selection went more quickly than Mr. Butler had expected because most of the prospective members indicated that they had heard little, if anything, about the case prior to the trial. That was not really surprising, since the local news outlets, including the daily paper, usually gave scant adverse publicity to the Sheriff's department if the latter was involved in an issue that raised any controversy.

Consequently, the group was empaneled by the morning of the second day of the trial.

During his career, Dr. Lyons had presented forensic findings to jurors literally hundreds of times, and in the process he found that some of the most effective strategies involved showing the pathology at the end of the plaintiff's case. This information, and particularly the pictures, tended to get their attention more quickly than almost anything else during the trial.

The introductory statements by the attorneys for both the Freemans and the defense were made on the afternoon of the second day, and by the next morning it was time to start calling witnesses. With Kevin Butler opening the proceedings, that would consist of eliciting testimony from each of the people he called to testify, whereupon they would each be cross-examined by the defense.

Most of the eyewitnesses told basically the same story indicating that they had seen the victim exit his vehicle and disappear into the woods. They seemed unsure of whether or not anyone hit or injured him.

Mr. Deveraux, however, gave an account of seeing several officers drag him from the car, "hitting Mr. Freeman several times, and dragging him into the woods. The man's legs were just dragging behind him like he was paralyzed!" he offered. To which the defense immediately objected that his testimony was "speculative." But the judge overruled the objection.

On cross-examination the defense attorney asked how clear was his recollection of the incident. Mr. Deveraux replied he had repeated the story a number of times, including the "three times the police came to my house asking questions about it!"

The defense attorney knew that he was in dangerous territory when questioning this witness, because if he even alluded to the details of Deveraux's memory of the incident, the existence of the cell-phone video could be revealed.

If the defense brought it up, they might open the door, allowing the video to be entered into evidence. Consequently, the attorney decided to terminate the cross-examination at that point.

The police expert Reginald Baker was on the stand for a total of forty-five minutes, basically reiterating for the jury what proper law-enforcement actions would be in situations such as the stopping and arresting of Henry Freeman. Attorney Butler proposed several hypothetical questions regarding possible misconduct, to which the defense responded that they were irrelevant since none of those actions had occurred in this case. The defense basically denied that anyone had done anything wrong, and that Freeman drowned while trying to escape.

Court was adjourned early on the third day following that testimony, and Dr. Lyons was scheduled to testify the next morning at nine o'clock. However, the start was delayed because of the absence of one of the jurors, a middle-aged African-American female school teacher, who was serving on a jury for the first time.

When she finally arrived at the Courthouse and was questioned by the judge who began to admonish her for her tardiness. At this point, she related the story of having been stopped by one of the local Sheriff's deputies while on route to court. She had been detained by the side of the road for about thirty minutes while he checked her driver's license and vehicle registration and ultimately allowed to continue, with no reason given for the traffic stop.

During the entire proceedings up to that point, the gallery had been filled with deputies from the Sheriff's Department. All of them showed up in full uniform including their service revolvers, which were prominently displayed for everyone, including the jurors, to see.

The incident involving the juror, however, apparently prompted a call from the federal judge in charge of the trial to someone in the law-enforcement community. After that, there were no further incidents, and the number of armed deputies in the audience diminished somewhat.

Clearly, this attempt at juror intimidation could not be so easily remedied. While Kevin Butler reluctantly considered moving for a mistrial, he calculated that the Judge would allow the trial to continue anyway, and decided to proceed with his case.

It was after lunch when Arthur Lyons finally made it to the stand, and Mr. Butler began his questioning. He began with an elaboration of the training and experience necessary to become a forensic pathologist, after which he was accepted as an expert in the field. This was despite several objections from the defense, attempting to question his credentials and insinuating that he was not qualified because wasn't the "official Medical Examiner" involved in the case. The objections were immediately overruled, and the testimony begun.

The first and most-important finding from the standpoint of the juror's understanding of the mechanism by which the victim drowned was the presentation of the findings. This included the photographs from both the first and second autopsies, and how and why it was that a second examination was even performed.

"I was called in by the family to review the case because they were very concerned that this wasn't a simple drowning," Lyons began. "The first autopsy had been done by the Medical Examiner and showed heavy lungs due to fluid in air sacs—a typical finding in a drowning case."

Proceeding to explain the mechanism of what occurs when an individual drowns, Lyons showed several photos of the lung taken thru the microscope to illustrate his testimony.

"The main concern was that the press had been told, by the police, that Mr. Freeman jumped into the water and drowned because he couldn't swim. In fact, he was not only an excellent swimmer, but he owned a scuba diving business in the Bahamas—hardly the description of a non-swimmer! So at that point his sister called me to come down and do another examination."

Lyons went on to explain that when he initially examined the body at the Medical Examiner's office, the other organs that had been removed showed no evidence of any significant disease processes going on. But several areas, including the spinal column in the chest and the back of the neck, had not been dissected.

"Doctor Lyons," Butler continued, "is there any particular reason you decided to conduct a more extensive dissection that the Medical Examiner had done?"

"Well in my experience I've seen a number of cases where a blow to the back, particularly in the upper back or neck, caused significant trauma, even though nothing was visible from the outside—just looking at the skin." Lyons answered. "If there is any severe trauma to that area, it can cause a temporary paralysis to occur, and that may prove to be fatal if a person is in an environment such as water—where even a good swimmer might drown."

"So, what did you discover?" the attorney continued.

"When we opened the skin, which looked normal from the outside, we found a large area of fresh hemorrhage around the vertebrae of the lower neck and upper thoracic region. As we continued the dissection, we found some blood around the spinal cord itself."

Anticipating the next question, Lyons continued, "There was no bruising or scraping of the skin in the back that we'd expect if Mr. Freeman struck something while sliding down the embankment of the canal, so the findings were most consistent with a compression-type force being applied to the area—perhaps a 'knee-drop' to a person lying on the ground."

Asked if he had seen this type of injury before, the pathologist indicated that he had, on a number of different occasions, the most common being while law enforcement officers were making an arrest. And while the majority of these cases involved unintentional injury inflicted during a physical altercation, "a few cases appeared to be less than accidental—or at least were the result of excessive force."

The defense attorneys immediately objected to the last part of his testimony as being speculative, and the Judge sustained the objection—but the jury had already heard it and understood the significance of that statement.

"Doctor Lyons," Mr. Butler continued alluding to the photos showing the areas of injured muscle and soft tissue as well as the pictures from the microscopic slides showing blood infiltrating into the tissues from disrupted blood vessels. These photos were proof that these changes were not 'post-mortem artifact' as Dr. Stanton had opined. "What, in your opinion, is the manner of death?"

"In my opinion, this should be classified as a homicide, because I believe Mr. Freeman was injured during an altercation with the police resulting in partial paralysis due to shock of the spinal cord. When he ended up in the water, he was unable to use his arms and legs at least temporarily and subsequently drowned," Lyons responded.

There were surprisingly few objections from the opposite side during Dr. Lyons' testimony—a situation that was, in his experience, somewhat unusual, but not totally unexpected in the setting of a civil lawsuit.

During the early years after retiring from the Medical Examiner's office and consulting for attorneys representing a defendant in Criminal cases, he often encountered the strategy of constant interruption by opposing counsel when attempting to fully explain a concept or finding to the jury.

Every time he would begin to explain an answer proffered by the Defense, the State attorney would voice an objection—often before his answer was even complete. In most instances, the objection would be overruled, but it still had the effect of chopping-up the testimony, with the clear intent of making it less understandable to those jurors.

These tactics proved totally ineffective, and after a while were generally abandoned, although it was always frustrating for any forensic scientist whose training and basic mission was to provide accurate and objective scientific evidence. Members of a jury who were, for the most part, not knowledgeable in rather specialized areas being discussed would have lawyers treat them as adversarial—the exact opposite of what the introduction of science into the courtroom was meant to accomplish.

Lyons had developed a fairly effective strategy in dealing with these instances. After determining that the jury was being annoyed by the constant interruptions and wanted to hear his side of the story, he simply would remain silent after a question from the State. Upon being prompted to answer, he would simply say, "Oh, I thought there was an objection!" This tactic almost always prompted laughter from the jury, and eventually led the State to the recognition that this was not a particularly fruitful approach for them to undertake and occasionally, it forced them to actually address the facts of the case.

There was a rather wide-spread opinion within the community of scientists and doctors that the greatest danger facing Forensic Science came from the Prosecutors who would often attempt to discredit and subjugate any factual data—regardless of how accurate it was—when it did not comport with their theory, solely for the purpose of winning the case.

"If they keep this up, the public will lose confidence in the science and facts won't matter anymore in the courtroom," Arthur Lyons had told Kevin Butler prior to the trial, as he had opined to many other attorneys in the past. "Let's see how our favorite Medical Examiner handles this on the stand!"

They didn't have long to wait, as it turned out, because he was the third witness for the defense following Lyons' testimony and the Plaintiff's lawyer resting his case.

Ahead of Dr. Stanton, the defense had called two of the police officers who had responded to the scene that night. Both of them were supervisors who testified that they had reviewed the records from the incident and found no irregularities. Henry Freeman had apparently jumped into the canal while attempting to elude officers making a lawful arrest—end of case!

Interestingly enough, there were no clear records of the identity of the officers that actually were observed by the eye-witnesses apparently striking and then dragging Freeman into the woods. These were events that the police representatives continued to insist never happened.

Because of this, the Plaintiff's lawyer had not been able to pinpoint specific individuals and was forced to bring suit against the entire department as an entity. This probably turned out to be more beneficial since obviously there wasn't going to be any effort by the State to hold any one individual responsible—regardless of the outcome of the family's legal efforts.

In the review of the police records, however, Kevin Butler was able to obtain the recorded logs regarding the utilization of the Tazers issued to each of the officers. This was mandatory documentation of the times at which any specific weapon was discharged, and he could ascertain for certain that at least two devices showed evidence of being used at or around the time of the confrontation with Henry Freeman.

Although the specific location where these electrical discharges were made couldn't be documented, the circumstances along with the law-enforcement dash-cam videos—which were admitted on the basis of being public records as opposed to the images from Mr. Deveraux's cell-phone—documented with certainty that an altercation took place, despite the attempts of the Sheriff to refute it.

Ultimately both representatives from law enforcement had to admit under oath that there was some contact between several deputies and the victim, but they continued to insist that no significant injuries had resulted from those interactions.

At this point, it became apparent that the results from the two autopsies would be the most determinative factors in the entire proceedings. Lyons and Butler awaited the anticipated testimony of the Medical Examiner, and although Dr. Don Kacey had actually performed the first autopsy, the chief Medical Examiner Geoffrey Stanton was, to everyone's surprise, the one called by the defense to testify regarding the results of the first autopsy.

"Doc," Kevin Butler texted to Arthur Lyons when Stanton walked into the courtroom. "They called Stanton first. What in the hell is going on?"

Lyons, as an expert consultant, technically would have had the opportunity to actually sit in the courtroom in an advisory capacity to consult with Plaintiff's counsel. He never liked the idea of doing this for the simple reason that as a forensic scientist his function was to analyze the facts independently and render as objective an opinion as he could based on the information he had available.

This approach, which from the standpoint of professionalism was most appropriate, also helped create increased credibility with the jurors. He did not, for instance, read the depositions of other experts—on either side—as was done almost universally by experts on the other side.

He would always reiterate to the jury that he, as a scientist, was not there to refute others' opinions, but to analyze the facts and remain neutral. This was a position not taken by experts from the other side who almost always had read and critiqued Dr. Lyons' opinions, exhibiting a partisan approach as opposed to objective neutrality—a distinction not lost on jurors in most situations.

Although Butler had taken the depositions of both Drs. Kacey and Stanton, it was expected that the former, because he had actually performed the autopsy, would present those findings initially. Dr. Stanton would provide additional comments, possibly in rebuttal to Lyons testimony—obviously after having first reviewed that information for the sole purpose of providing contradictory opinions.

In his deposition Dr. Kacey had been somewhat evasive when discussing the autopsy findings. He was particularly evasive about the dissection performed by Lyons, which he actually attended—observing the evidence of blunt force trauma directly, in the autopsy room. He had admitted that the findings were real but was unwilling to offer an opinion as how they might have occurred. But importantly, he did not contradict any of the findings stating that he had not read any reports or statements, including depositions, given by anyone else.

On the witness stand questioned by Mr. Butler and then cross-examined by the Defense, Kacey went through his autopsy findings in a matter-of-fact manner without any reference—one way or another—to the traumatic injuries that would be uncovered later. Additionally, he wouldn't refute any of the opinions of Dr. Lyons when asked to do so.

The upshot of this would be a problem for the defense attorney since he didn't give them any ammunition that they could use to discredit the findings of the second autopsy. In the process, he actually had bolstered the credibility of Arthur Lyons.

Because the lawyers operated in an adversarial world while the doctors operated in the world of factual scientific data, there was always an underlying conflict during the introduction of science-based testimony in the courtroom.

The pathologists who performed both the first and second autopsies were seemingly pretty much in agreement—or at least not overtly contradictory—regarding each other's findings. And this situation was not tenable for a Defense that desperately needed testimony that would refute those findings.

Enter Dr. Geoffrey Stanton.

Although as a routine part of discovery Stanton's deposition had been taken earlier, both the attorney and Dr. Lyons were well-aware that surprises can happen during the course of the trial. Issues often arise that were totally unanticipated. The deposition usually brought out the general range of opinions that an expert would give, but sometimes important nuances would come out during testimony arising from variations of an attorney's questioning.

If a particular general area of potential testimony wasn't addressed during the pre-trial discovery deposition, the Judge might not allow an expert to testify about it in Court. But invariably specific issues within those general areas would surface during questioning at trial, and generally the expert would be allowed to opine on those, even though they had not been specifically addressed as a part of the discovery.

Because Dr. Stanton had only been called by the Defense, his initial testimony took place after the Plaintiff—the family represented by Kevin Butler—had presented their case and basically rested. After his presentation, the Plaintiff would of course have the opportunity to cross-examine.

"Dr. Stanton," lead Defense attorney Patrick O'Brien began. "Your office investigated and performed an autopsy on the body of Mr. Freeman after he jumped into a drainage canal and drowned, is that correct?"

Kevin Butler immediately objected to the question, asserting that the question was based on the assumption that the victim had indeed "jumped into the canal," alleged 'facts' that were clearly not proven by anything in evidence. And while the judge sustained the objection, the idea that this was, somehow the fault of Henry Freeman had been planted in the minds of the jurors.

While those jurors may be admonished to disregard those statements, human nature dictates that there will be some inferences that may, even if not consciously recognized, influence their later determinations.

Basically, the cat is out of the bag and it's hard to put it back in!

"Yes I did," was the initial response from the Chief Medical Examiner. "The case occurred in our jurisdiction, and consequently an investigator was sent to the scene to recover the body. Ultimately we did an autopsy on the body to determine the cause of death—which I determined to be drowning.

"Well Doctor Stanton," the attorney continued, "did you actually perform the autopsy?" To which the doctor responded that one of his subordinates had done the dissection, but he, as Chief Medical Examiner had supervised the case. He was the person who makes the final decision on any case, whoever performed the actual autopsy.

"And Doctor," he continued. "What were your conclusions after reviewing the autopsy performed by Dr. Kacey?"

"The findings included a large amount of frothy fluid in the lungs and some sandy material in the mouth and nose; very characteristic of a drowning, so I called it a drowning, plain and simple," was the Medical Examiner's reply.

The question of trauma came up next and Dr. Stanton continued.

"When we open the chest and abdomen we can see all the tissues of a person's back, so we were able to observe that there was no trauma of any significance—so that made it an accident."

As the testimony continued for a few more minutes the defense was making it increasingly clear that the strategy was essentially to ignore the findings of the second autopsy, simply dismissing Lyons' findings as post-mortem artifact. Of course the defense attorney was content with that explanation—and counted on the jury basically to fail to appreciate the significance of the trauma that had been previously demonstrated and ignore the science, which they had repeatedly characterized as 'fake' or 'biased.'

As Plaintiff's Attorney Kevin Butler stood up to begin the cross-examination of the Medical Examiner he began to realize that he'd been given a present by the Defense attorney. The pathologist was not asked any direct questions about the additional dissections that were needed to uncover the actual injuries to the back. Dr. Lyons opined this was a major contributing factor in the death.

"Dr. Stanton," Butler began. "Is it true that you were in the room when Dr. Arthur Lyons performed a second autopsy on the body of Henry Freeman?"

"Well, I was in and out of the room, and I saw a little bit of it but not the entire procedure," Stanton replied.

"Did Dr. Lyons not call you into the room and specifically show you the areas of hemorrhage after he had opened the skin on the back?" Butler continued the inquiry.

"I think he did at one point show me some areas he thought was bleeding, but I'm a little hazy on the details—it's been a while, you know."

"But Doctor, you've had a chance to review all the photos from both autopsies and discuss the case with Dr. Kacey, haven't you?" Butler pressed Stanton for a reply.

"Dr. Kacey was only a year or so out of his training program and was a pretty inexperienced doctor at the time. That's why he agreed with Dr. Lyons about the meaning of the blood around the spinal cord," Stanton replied.

Stanton had just confirmed, in front of the jury, a fact that previously had not been firmly established due to Kacey's waffling on the stand—that his associate, Dr. Kacey, had agreed with Lyons' findings in the room at the time of the dissection.

Apparently Dr. Stanton didn't appreciate the full implications of his revelation, and concluded his direct testimony with a few references to the inexperienced and "just out of training" status of the associate pathologist Stanton himself had hired. Stanton had allowed him to do all types of cases, including over ten homicide cases in which he had testified as an expert pathologist for the State.

Butler concluded by asking, "Well, Dr. Stanton, are you telling the jury that the convictions in these homicide cases are in question because of the inexperience of Dr. Kacey—maybe the verdicts should be thrown out?"

One of the defense attorneys for the County finally woke up to the now precipitous problem being raised by Butler's questioning. He jumped to his feet to offer an objection—to which the Judge asked, "what grounds?" But he did not hear any good reason why the Medical Examiner couldn't answer a simple question about an employee he had hired, and he over-ruled the objection.

Prompted again to answer the question, Dr. Stanton responded that "Dr. Kacey is an excellent pathologist, and his diagnoses are always correct—except this time!"

The response from the audience in the courtroom gallery, as well as the jury was a palpable effort to avoid all-out laughter. Most perceived that it wouldn't comport with accepted behavior in the courtroom, but it was all everyone could do to contain themselves.

The case was effectively over.

The Verdict & Aftermath

After about three hours of deliberation—including a lunch break—the jury came in with a verdict of five million dollars for the children of Henry Freeman. Included on the verdict form was as decision that the law enforcement investigation of the incident was not sufficient, and they recommended further investigation "to determine whether or not a crime had been committed."

One of the most damning facts to come to surface was what came to be recognized as an obvious cover-up by the office of the Medical Examiner. Because it was a public agency, it had always been assumed by the public to be above political influence.

That perception was obviously inaccurate as this case had demonstrated. This led to the realization, at least in this one community, that science was subject to the whims of politics—a fact that could ultimately undermine the public confidence in the entire field of forensic science in the courtroom.

Needless to say, Arthur Lyons had, for a number of years been concerned with precisely that issue. The effects of outside biases could affect the integrity of the scientific data utilized by the legal system wherein the scientist, an impartial observer, and the lawyer, operating in an adversarial legal system, attempt to coordinate their respective positions without altering the factual truths involved.

While in theory that coordination should always result in an accurate depiction of the scientific information to the jurors, in realty that sometimes remained an elusive goal. Accuracy suffers particularly if the lawyers try to color facts in a way to be unduly prejudicial in favor of their case.

It isn't unusual, unfortunately, for an attorney, most often from the Prosecution, to attempt to subtly manipulate the scientific data in a way that would further the attempt to prove his or her case.

Although the exercise of this influence usually wouldn't be so overt as to directly confront the doctor or forensic scientist performing laboratory testing, more subtle instances could occur. Examples include a supervisor in a Crime Lab telling a technician that he or she wasn't coming up with enough positive results on tests requiring interpretation, or a detective telling a forensic pathologist their theory of what happened while the doctor was in the middle of performing an autopsy on a suspected victim of a criminal assault.

In those situations, the message subtly conveyed was that there would be fewer complications if the forensic analysis turned out to be consistent with the law enforcement and prosecutors view of the particular case. These kinds of suggestions could easily progress to intimidations.

The verdict in the death of Henry Freeman resulted in a significant monetary award for the family—providing for the future of his children—but did little to effect any change in the culture of the law enforcement community in this small coastal

Florida community. Despite the recommendations of the jury, it did not trigger any new investigations into the potential criminal aspects of the incident in the canal.

The 'good-old-boy' network was alive and well on the Florida coast.

One of the first evidences of possible retaliation occurred when Dr. Don Kacey received stellar performance evaluations from Dr. Stanton—evaluations that Larry often called the "kiss of death" when was working for the County. Dr. Kacey was terminated at the end of the year when his Medical Examiner certificate from the State of Florida was not renewed.

"Doc," Larry asked, "Did you hear that the associate doctor got let go because the Medical Examiner Commission didn't renew his appointment?"

"No, I didn't know. When did that happen?" Lyons inquired.

"Just last week. I heard it from one of the guys in the office down there." Larry replied.

Although Larry had only spent a total of three hours of his life in that Medical Examiner's office. at the time of the second autopsy, he had managed to develop a highly-functional network of interactions with the autopsy technicians. These were folks that had a real handle on what was going on in the office. Consequently, they had stayed in close contact with all the political intrigue that was going on.

"I could 'a told you this was going to happen," Larry continued. "The doc didn't testify the way they told him to!"

While Arthur Lyons was no stranger to this type of political retaliation it still came as a complete and somewhat disturbing surprise that the State had become involved in the situation.

It was certainly not unexpected that a local doctor would run afoul of the local political establishment while trying honestly to do his or her job, but it was of considerable concern that it would become an issue at the State level. This indicated the existence of political influence beyond the local environment.

"How in the hell did the State get involved?" Lyons demanded.

"I guess these guys have more pull than we gave them credit for," was Larry's response. "The guys tell me that there was a real fight in the office. They all thought Dr. Kacey was a really good pathologist and was just telling the truth, but he still got screwed!"

To Arthur Lyons this was all "déjà vu all over again" as the saying goes.

Many years ago during a stint with a County Medical Examiner's office, he had been asked to cover up a case involving a young lady arrested on a drug charge. After being released from the Emergency Room of a local hospital, with prescription medications to manage possible drug withdrawal and instructions as to how to administration those medications, she was placed in a cell and denied any medications.

The result was a seizure and death, which was reported to the Medical Examiner in virtue of her being in custody.

Arthur Lyons had performed the autopsy and determined the death to be the result of negligence due to deliberate withholding of prescribed medications by the jailers. This triggered a lawsuit against the County for negligent homicide.

The chief Medical Examiner was contacted by the County administration and told to have Dr. Lyons modify the cause of death to something that wouldn't blame the jail, in view of the pending lawsuit, but he refused. Subsequently he was harassed incessantly by the administration—including them lodging a complaint with their own professional affairs committee.

The in-house committee found no proof of any wrong-doing but reported that "although there is no proof, there might be the perception that there were activities potentially decremental to the County." Still, they offered no disciplinary actions probably resulting from the knowledge of their totally untenable position.

Because he realized that this retaliation would most likely go on indefinitely as long as he was in the employ of the County, Arthur Lyons turned in his resignation and started into full-time private practice. He performed private autopsies, directed several diagnostic pathology officers and provided consultation services in the area of forensic medicine and pathology. This was a practice that turned out to be much more rewarding in virtually all aspects of the endeavor.

He had departed voluntarily, documenting some of the problems in the office. This revelation led to an investigation of the chief Medical Examiner by the State Attorney's office that resulted in his ultimate dismissal. Still, Arthur Lyons was often questioned in court about his 'firing' from the office, necessitating him to spend more time than he wanted in going through the entire episode.

Since it turned out that in most instances the jurors immediately recognized the problems with the governmental organizations and regarded Dr. Lyons to be clearly in the right, after a few years the situation with the Medical Examiner's office was rarely broached by any attorney from either side of a case.

Because of his experience with similar issues and feeling that Dr. Kacey had really gotten screwed in this process, Arthur Lyons had contacted the now unemployed pathologist and given some fatherly advice. "You won't be able to stay away from the politicos, but don't ever capitulate to them or you won't survive —professionally or personally."

Despite all the negative fallout after the verdict, it was important to remember that the family of Henry Freeman had actually prevailed in the case. This fact was only reluctantly acknowledged by either the County or the press corps who seemingly had gone out of their way to avoid any coverage that would, in any way, inform the public of what was going on.

It was an ongoing problem that the pathologist had experienced many times during his career, wherein issues of significant legal importance would be essentially ignored by the local media outlets—including television and the newspapers—limiting the opportunity for the general public to become even aware, let alone informed! And it was always a challenge to inform people who, for the most part, were seemingly disinterested in those issues—or at least were ill-informed as to their significance.

Arthur Lyons had been involved in an important case early in his career when he challenged the State of Georgia, which at the time was utilizing non-physician pharmacists to provide Medical Examiner services in criminal cases. While clearly they were not doctors—or even medically-trained technicians—they were portraying themselves as forensic pathologists when performing autopsies and testifying as experts in the courtroom.

After providing information and testimony to the state legislature, Lyons, then working as a pathologist in the local hospital and providing forensic pathology services to the local Coroner, was dismissed from his volunteer position by those same individuals. They just happened to be the directors of the state Crime Laboratory and had been given the power to appoint doctors around the state as Medical Examiners.

The ensuing lawsuit addressed many important issues, including the fact that unqualified people had been making decisions that resulted in individuals receiving long prison terms —and even in a few cases execution—based upon totally fabricated data generated by unqualified 'forensic scientists!'

While the civil trial ended up with the jury ruling against them on the narrow issue of whether the State acted unlawfully in Lyons' dismissal, there was enough momentum generated within the legal community to essentially end the existing system and replace the pharmacists with qualified forensically trained pathologists.

This represented a major step forward in the development of a science-based medicolegal investigative system, but there was virtually no reference to the case in any of the public media channels. It was presumed that the public would not be interested in such mundane issues related to their Constitutional rights.

Apparently, that judgement by the press was a self-fulling prophecy!

Dr. Lyons' admonition to the fledgling pathologist was simply to "stick to your guns," remembering that this type of attack had become almost an occupational hazard for forensic scientists. But Dr. Lacey apparently decided that he had had enough and accepted a position with a large commercial laboratory with three times the income and none of the political pressure he had experienced as Medical Examiner.

"Larry," Lyons pointed out. They were once again in the middle of opening the chest of a middle-aged woman found dead in her flat after not having been seen at work for several days—exposing a massive hemorrhage in the pericardium (the sack around the heart) resulting from a myocardial infarction in the left ventricle of the heart. She had been sent home from the hospital emergency room the day before with a diagnosis of 'indigestion.' "We lost another good pathologist to the system."

"Doc, I've always told you that the system is just screwed-up no matter how you slice it. They're always going to look out for theirselves and screw anybody else!"

C'mon Larry," the pathologist responded. "Don't look at everything like it was the end of the world. We did win this case you know?"

"Yeah. But why did they send this poor lady home from the Emergency Room?" Larry said, pointing to the blood-filled pericardium on the body they were dissecting. "They really missed the boat on this one—again."

Lyons had to step back a bit. He was again surprised and all the while impressed by his associate's totally pragmatic approach to his cases—and life in general. It was an approach he longingly wished he could emulate.

Case Study #3

The Case of the Angel of Death

The Discovery of a Dilemma

Dr. Arthur Lyons and his forensic technologist assistant Larry Hudson were in the middle of an autopsy of a fairly young-looking sixty-four year old gentleman. He had been found dead in his hospital bed early in the morning of the day he was supposed to be discharged, and because the family was concerned they had requested an autopsy to find out what happened.

Mr. Howard Campbell had been admitted for issues related to his pacemaker that began while vacationing in Central Florida from his home in New York. He had noticed an unusual sound emanating from the device, although there didn't seem to be a problem as far as he could tell.

After he presented himself to the Emergency Room at a local hospital, he was initially seen by an ER doctor who ultimately sought a consultation from a Cardiologist to further evaluate the problem.

This type of referral is not uncommon in the hospital setting. Most of the physicians are either employed by or have contracts with the hospital, and a hierarchy of referrals has been established. While having the potential for enhanced patient care because of the immediate availability of many specialties, it also had the downside for potential abuse by generating consultations that are not medically indicated or completely necessary but do generate increased income for the institution.

"Doc," Larry turned to the pathologist. "I got the pacemaker out and all the wires, and they look ok."

"Thanks Larry,' Lyons responded. "Great job!"

While the pathologist performed most of the dissection during a autopsy, there were some areas in which the tech was invaluable. These areas included sawing open the skull to allow examination of the brain and tracing such things as pacemaker wires through the veins to the heart. The tech provided a second set of hands while the ends of the wires were being examined by the pathologist on the other end.

"This guy doesn't look too bad, Doc," he said, as the heart was removed and placed on the scale. "Four-hundred-twenty grams. Looks a little big but not anything serious."

"Larry, I know you're a genius, but let's take look inside before you get too excited," was the reply.

Lyons followed the path of the coronary arteries coursing along the front and then back surfaces of the heart. While noting a small amount of localized calcification—not uncommon in a man in his sixties—he saw no areas of narrowing as might be the case in severe coronary artery disease.

"Larry, see this crunchy area?" Lyons pointed to a fairly rigid but completely open section of the large vessel coursing down the front of the left ventricle of the heart. "This calcification is common in older people but usually just an incidental finding and doesn't mean much. These guys advertising the scans that are supposed to pick up disease are just picking up these little bits of calcium—don't mean anything, but they're making a fricking fortune!"

"Just another con job" Larry responded. "So, what's the story with this guy?" pointing to the middle-aged-looking man on the autopsy table.

Larry wasn't the only one that was beginning to wonder about the findings in the autopsy they were performing. In most situations, the cause of death was obvious at some point. It was usually either a blood clot to the lung, a thrombosis in one of the coronary arteries, an area of bleeding into the brain or from an aneurysm either in the chest or the abdomen.

This time, however, aside from a significant amount of fluid in the lung—pulmonary edema, indicating an acute terminal heart failure which could result from many conditions—they weren't finding much in the way of a definitive diagnosis. There wasn't a "smoking-gun" finding that would explain the sudden and unexpected death of this man in the circumstance wherein it had occurred.

As they dissected the various organs, there were some minor findings, such as a moderately enlarged heart and prostatic hypertrophy, but no underlying lung or kidney disease. Certainly there were no abrupt changes such as a blood clot in one of the coronary arteries that would explain his sudden deterioration and death.

As Medical Examiner, Arthur Lyons had had many cases of sudden unexpected death during his long career. Often an apparent cause became evident during the actual dissection part of the autopsy, but in at least thirty-to-forty percent of the time, further investigation would be necessary. This would include the examination of the tissues under the microscope and testing blood and other body fluids, such as urine, for drugs and toxic substances that might shine further light on the causality of the event.

Over the years, many forensic pathologists had come to minimize the use of histology—the examination of tissues under the microscope. This was due to the mistaken impression that they could make most diagnoses using only the naked eye.

An unfortunate statement was made by a well-known Medical Examiner in the setting of an international gathering of pathologists. He said something to the effect that his "diagnoses were made using the telephone rather than the microscope," referring to the idea of gathering information about the circumstances of a death from law enforcement, witnesses and the like. He indicated this information would supersede any data gained by using the microscope, further re-enforcing his somewhat tenuous theory.

The result of this was that a major component of pathology practice, the evaluation of tissues under the microscope—while the basis of practice in the pathology community dealing with patient diagnosis thru evaluation of biopsy specimens—became to be largely marginalized in the practice of forensic pathology, with the emphasis being placed upon information gathering.

While the consideration of data regarding an event is important, the potential for the introduction of incorrect information—either accidentally or by intent—create a significant risk. If the pathologist depends upon that information as the basis of their diagnosis, he could reach the wrong conclusions. There is, instead, the hard scientific reality afforded by the actual examination of the tissues.

This mind-set, obviously, was a self-fulfilling prophesy because the pathologists would never know what diagnoses they were missing since they didn't look!

To further complicate the situation, for a long time the pathologist tended to take the information provided over the phone usually by law enforcement at face value. Only recently have they begun to appreciate the fact that in many instances this data was not completely objective. Oft times it was colored by the subjectivity and biases inherent in any observations—including those from supposedly neutral law enforcement sources.

And indeed, Dr. Lyons had uncovered many such errors when performing second autopsies. Second autopsies following an initial Medical Examiner examination have discovered such things as infections in the heart or brain, early infarctions in the heart, brain or lung due to interrupted blood flow, and diffuse blood disease such as leukemia—undetectable to the naked eye.

Needless to say, the Medical Examiner community reacted as expected. They denigrated the subsequent information as inconsequential or erroneous, rather than treating it as a learning experience. They weren't recognizing that the microscope was a vital part of forensic practice, as it was in the clinical and hospital setting—where the evaluation of tissue biopsies under the microscope represented a critical part of making a proper diagnosis.

Because of his forensic background, Lyons was more aware of the possibility of drugs and toxic agents playing a part in these types of death—an area that was almost universally ignored by pathologists practicing in the hospital setting. It was not only unusual, but almost unheard of for a hospital autopsy to include analysis of blood for toxicology analysis.

The duality of his roles and training in both hospital and forensic arenas provided a somewhat unique perspective when approaching these types of situations, often leading up to a more complete analysis than would have taken place in either of the other settings.

Upon finding little evidence of a readily-apparent cause for the death of this seemingly healthy individual at the autopsy, Dr. Lyons realized that the answers would most likely be forthcoming from either the microscopic exam of the tissues or from the toxicology results from the testing of the blood and urine.

"Larry, I'm going to need at least 20 cassettes," Lyons indicated to his tech, referring to the small plastic containers into which small pieces of tissue would be placed after being preserved in a formaldehyde solution. They would be sent to the lab where thin slices would be cut and placed on a glass slide, stained with a blue and red dye, and prepared for examination under the microscope.

"Ok Doc, I've got them all labeled and have some blood tubes too," was the response.

The blood collection tubes were utilized in cases wherein a suspicion arose regarding the potential need for toxicology testing.

This would require the collection of not only blood, but other fluids such as urine and bile from the gallbladder. These would have value in determining whether or not any drugs or medications were in any way contributory to the death. In some situations, even the fluid from the interior of the eye—the vitreous—could be of value, particularly for determining of the electrolytes in the system at the time of death.

"You realize Doc," Larry continued. "This is a hospital case, do you think we need tox?"

"Larry, I thought you'd seen enough of these cases to know better!" Lyons responded jokingly. "Just because the hospital guys don't do it, you think we don't need to?"

Both Larry and the pathologist were well-aware of the necessity for a complete analysis. In too many instances where second examinations following a hospital autopsy had been done, serious questions regarding medication and drugs had been raised. But because no samples had been taken during the original procedure, and most of the blood had been lost down the drain during the procedure, no testing could be performed subsequently.

Obtaining a suitable sample required placing a needle in one of the large veins, usually in the lower abdomen and drawing a sample into a syringe. This sample would then be placed into a collection tube where it would be stored until the desired testing would be performed.

In order to limit possible contamination, the blood would be drawn during the first part of the autopsy, immediately after opening the skin and exposing the insides of the chest and abdomen. Samples of urine and bile would also be taken at this time—after which the dissection of the organs would begin.

The dissection part of the autopsy was finished in about two hours during which there had been no findings visible to the naked eye that would explain the sudden downhill course the patient took leading to his death.

At this point, the pathologist could only wait for the microscopic slides to come back from the lab for his review. He also awaited the results of the toxicology testing he had ordered to be performed on the blood and urine.

Meanwhile, the funeral home had been pressing for a determination of cause of death in order to file a Death Certificate with the State: protocol called for filing within five days of the death. And although in many situations that cause is obvious, on some occasions, such as this, it would be necessary to wait for all the information to become available—including the toxicology results.

While the death certificate was generally perceived by the general public as being authoritative, the truth was that in many cases, particularly if an autopsy had not been performed, the information that a physician listed was really an educated guess based upon the information he or she had on the patient.

Arthur Lyons had experienced this situation on numerous occasions. Many times, he performed an autopsy after a doctor had already signed off on a death only to discover a totally unexpected process that had actually caused the demise.

Many people, not only in the general public but within the medical profession itself, failed to appreciate the possibility that much of the health-related information regarding mortality rates was based on erroneous information. This happens particularly on issues related to heart disease where the physician would often call a death a heart attack or cardiac arrest simply to complete the paperwork and satisfy State reporting requirements.

Because the family was particularly concerned that the death not only was sudden but also had occurred in hospital, they had specifically requested the pathologist to sign the Death Certificate rather than the attending physician at the hospital—understanding that there would be somewhat of a delay.

A Questionable Cause of Death

It usually took about ten days for the blood work and the tissue slides to come back from the laboratory and another day or so before Dr. Lyons had a chance to review the slides. At this point he observed significant amounts of edema fluid in the lungs that had developed suddenly as the result of respiratory failure.

Additionally, there were a few scattered areas of scarring in the heart muscle, but not enough recent change to account for the severity of the symptoms that were noted. There was certainly no evidence of an acute process such as a clot in a major artery or inflammation of the heart muscle.

The examination under the microscope of tissue taken at the autopsy would allow the pathologist to see changes not readily visible to the naked eye. He looked particularly for subtle evidence of early injury to the cells resulting from lack of blood flow or a possible infection.

He found no such evidence upon examining the tissue from every organ system. Only the tell-tale edema fluid in the lungs—still no concrete answers as to why this gentleman was dead!

"Hi, I'm just calling to find out if you want to have the Fentanyl quantitated as well as the other opioids," asked the supervisor in the toxicology lab on the phone.

"You found Fentanyl?" Dr. Lyons responded.

"Yes," she replied. "It appears that it's just the parent drug but we can't tell the levels at this point. So I wanted to find out if you wanted to quantitate."

The finding of a "parent" drug in the blood indicates that there had been no time for the drug to pass through the liver where it would be detoxified. In that case, metabolites of that drug would also be present in the sample. This allowed the pathologist to get an idea of how long prior to death it was administered, since all the metabolism ceased at the time of death.

Although the microscopic slides had arrived from the histology lab, the toxicology report had been delayed because of the further testing that needed to be done. While Lyons was a little surprised that anything at all was found, he authorized the lab to determine the levels of the drugs in question in order to ascertain whether or not they had played any part in the death.

As a part of the work-up of some cases, particularly when the patient had been hospitalized for any significant amount of time, it was Arthur Lyons' policy to obtain the medical records for review. This was a policy that often proved quite helpful in the determination of the cause of death.

Even during his stints with various Medical Examiner offices, the records often proved invaluable in understanding what was the patient's condition upon arrival and what treatments and medications were rendered. He also was able to review any x-rays, EKG's, and laboratory reports.

He also had found out early-on that the records received when a family requested them were not always accurate. His first experience involved the death of a forty-five-year-old woman found dead in her house. She had been seen in the local Emergency Room the previous evening, complaining of chest pain.

The diagnosis of anxiety attack was made after several hours spent in the waiting room and about fifteen minutes seeing the ER doctor. The patient sent home—where she was discovered deceased the next morning.

Because of the sudden death, the case was referred to the Medical Examiner's Office where an autopsy revealed the cause to be a pericardial tamponade—blood filling the sac around the heart compressing it to the point it can no longer function. This was the result of the rupture of a portion of the left ventricle that had been compromised following the formation of a clot occluding the coronary artery and interrupting the blood flow to that area.

Because the Medical Examiner investigator obtained a copy of the records at the time he picked up the body in the Emergency Room directly from hospital medical records department—in the middle of the night—they had not yet been reviewed by anyone in the department and represented the raw data generated regarding this patient.

Perhaps the most telling finding was an EKG strip that clearly showed changes that were virtually diagnostic of an acute myocardial infarction, wherein appropriate medical intervention would be indicated.

In the ensuing several weeks, questions arose from the family about the circumstances of the death, and they hired an attorney to help in their investigation. He subsequently looked into both the hospital and Medical Examiner records.

To Arthur Lyons, who had performed the autopsy and reviewed the hospital records as a part of his overall evaluation, the issue was fairly clear-cut: this woman died as the result of an untreated heart attack, and there was clear evidence of it in the medical records.

So, it came as no surprise when he was contacted by a lawyer representing the victim's family. The lawyer wanted to meet and discuss the findings of the autopsy which had just been completed, with receipt of the microscopic slides and the toxicology findings. This was the information that confirmed the heart muscle had been injured due to the interruption of blood flow, and that the changes obvious under the microscope were indicative of a myocardial infarction, or heart attack, that was 24- to 36-hours old—clearly present at the time she was in the Emergency Room.

Although many of the cases involving the Medical Examiner were related to violent deaths, a significant number of times the death proved to be natural and involved medical diseases such as coronary artery disease. This would open up the necessity for a thorough and complete evaluation of these processes.

Arthur Lyons was often dismayed by the attitudes of some of his more recently trained colleagues toward these types of cases. They would often perform fairly cursory examinations of these routine deaths. That would mean they could pay more attention to the more exciting cases such as homicides that they felt were more challenging to their professional expertise.

But he always tried to treat all the cases with the same degree of diligence. He never knew what might transpire in the future and wanted to have all the bases covered.

During his meeting with the attorney the family had engaged to look into the death of this relatively young, apparently healthy woman, the lawyer expressed surprise at the diagnosis provided by Lyons from the autopsy he indicated that he had reviewed the medical records that the family had requested from the hospital, and there was nothing in those records that would suggest a cardiac event.

At that point, Lyons went over the copy of the medical records provided to the lawyer only to discover that the electro-cardiogram that he had reviewed was noticeably absent—as was any reference to the ordering or reporting of that test. He realized that while the investigator had obtained the actual unaltered records, that was not the same as the official record generated for distribution to the family and their attorneys.

There was a County-instituted policy in the Medical Examiner's office that any records not actually generated by the office—records from an outside source such as the hospital—

could not be released as part of a public records request. They would need to be obtained directly from the institution.

Consequently, as Medical Examiner, he couldn't release the missing EKG data to the family's attorney although it was clearly pertinent to any potential legal action contemplated against the hospital. Under the rules, he shouldn't even inform the lawyer of the discrepancy. But Dr. Lyons didn't always follow the rules precisely, and those records were ultimately released to the family upon Court order in the malpractice lawsuit that followed. That lawsuit ended in a substantial verdict in their favor, augmented by a jury expressing their dissatisfaction with the clearly-evident cover-up attempt on the part of the hospital.

Dr. Lyons also learned a valuable lesson regarding the political intrigue that existed within the administrations of both the hospital and the county Medical Examiner's office.

A review of the records from Mr. Campbell's case revealed that he initially presented himself to the Emergency Room with no complaints of illness. He simply wanted to have an analysis of his pacemaker for any possible malfunction.

After being admitted to the hospital for a cardiology consult, a minor abnormality was discovered on an electrocardiogram. While he remained asymptomatic it was suggested that they perform a cardiac catheterization procedure while he was there, prior to being discharged.

The procedure had been performed successfully with no significant findings in the heart itself or the coronary arteries. But afterwards, over the period of the next three days, Mr. Campbell began to experience episodes of shortness of breath and periodic chest pain for which he was administered several pain medications—including a mild opioid—but no strong painkillers.

On the evening prior to the day he was to be discharged home, his wife called the charge nurse into the room indicating that he was acting differently. He appeared confused and did not recognize her when she had come in while another nurse was administering some medications into his IV.

The nurse's notes also included the wife's questioning as to what medication he had received, and the instructions were not to give him any of that again.

According to the nurses notes, Dr. Lyons was able to determine that Mr. Campbell's respirations were somewhat labored at that point and he remained confused, but appeared to the staff to be stable for the next few hours. After his wife had left the hospital for the night, ready to take him home the following morning, he suffered a cardiac arrest and a "code blue" was called to perform resuscitation.

The records indicated that he was found unresponsive by the team, lying in bed. At that point, he was intubated and cardiopulmonary resuscitation measures instituted, resulting in restoration of a heart beat and blood pressure. But he never regained consciousness.

His wife was called and returned to the hospital. After about five hours in the intensive care unit, she decided, on the advice of the attending doctor, to suspend further resuscitative efforts, despite her ongoing confusion as to what had happened so suddenly to cause her husband's demise. And now, as regards to confusion, so was Arthur Lyons!

In review of the records, looking particularly at the medication administration documentation, any reference to Fentanyl being signed out from the pharmacy and directed toward patient Campbell, could not be found. This prompted a concern that this potentially deadly drug had been administered in error.

Because Fentanyl was a well-known drug of abuse, tight controls were in place, most notably in the hospital setting. The drug was often utilized in the induction of anesthesia for surgical cases—with strict requirements for documentation of who the drug was intended for, and how much was being signed-out from Pharmacy.

Consequently, this presented a quandary to the pathologist. He wanted to get to the bottom of the questionable absence of records documentation while not appearing as an alarmist raising the issue of a potential drug-induced death—an accident, or possibly worse!

Problems would often arise with these cases, in determining exactly when the meds were given. Considering that this particular patient survived post-cardiac arrest for about five hours, during which he was in the intensive care unit and receiving a number of medications, the records showed no reference to Fentanyl.

After contacting the medical records and pharmacy departments on multiple occasions, Dr. Lyons finally received a response that the drug had been administered during resuscitation, with a single tablet placed beneath Campbell's tongue prior to the intubation. He was told that the record of this had been put on a separate "orders" page not included in the official medical records readout on the computer.

"Can you send me that page?" Lyons asked the records supervisor on the phone. "I have the written permission from the family."

"Sorry, I've checked with my supervisor, and that's not available for release at this time," was the reply.

Although Dr. Lyons had come up against some pretty unusual situations during his career, this refusal had to rank high on the exasperation scale—an eleven out of ten—particularly as there seemed to be no rationale for the decision.

After coming up against a veritable brick wall in attempting to resolve the dilemma, and because of a pretty clear law in Florida regarding the duty of all physicians to report any suspicious death to the proper authorities, Arthur Lyons contacted the local Medical Examiner's office to report his findings.

Several weeks had passed after sending the autopsy notes and reports, including the toxicology results from the blood drawn at autopsy, documenting a moderately high level of Fentanyl. In addition there was identification of several of the other drugs that had been documented as having been administered during the resuscitation. Lyons, having received no response, called the office to inquire as to the status of their investigation.

"Dr. Lyons, it's good to hear from you again," said Alicia Fernandez, a fellow pathologist and associate Medical Examiner at the district office. "How is everything with you?"

"Well I'm just following up to find out where we were on this guy with the Fentanyl. I sent it over a couple of weeks ago," was Lyons' reply.

"I was able to get in contact with the hospital, and they assured me that they had looked at everything, including the pharmacy records, and there was nothing out of the ordinary."

"Did they send you any documentation?" Lyons continued, now wanting to press her for obtaining the records that the hospital failed to produce to him.

"Well, no, actually," was the response. "They didn't send anything, but I got the confirmation verbally from the records supervisor that everything was copacetic."

Arthur Lyons was incredulous. "Alicia, what's going on? Why can't anybody just get the documentation that this was supposedly appropriately given during resuscitation?"

"I know, Arthur, that that's a problem, but our office isn't going to press the issue any further, according to my bosses," was the somewhat hesitant reply.

"Okay," he replied, "I'm beginning to see the picture here, and I understand your position. Thanks for your help."

As if he hadn't been suspicious before, the seemingly nonsensical behavior on the part of both the hospital and the Medical Examiner—in not demanding some sort of documentation for the administration of a controlled substance having potentially life-threatening consequences—appeared totally incomprehensible to Dr. Lyons as a scientist and forensic pathologist.

The question was now: "Where do we go from here?"

Pursuing the Elusive Truth

"Where do we go from here, Doctor Lyons?" was the first question asked by the family of Mr. Campbell. They had been informed of the positive blood results from the autopsy, the stone-walling from the hospital, and the subsequent disinterest in pursuing the case on the part of the Medical Examiner's office.

It was clear that the levels of the drug were well in excess of what would be expected if a normal healthy adult had a single tablet placed under the tongue. But this was an individual who had suffered a catastrophic cardiac event, during which there was an absence of the circulation of blood required to absorb the drug in the first place. The second issue was why would a drug usually administered to quiet a patient during the induction of anesthesia would need to be given to an already unconscious patient?

While it was the case that toxicology studies were almost never performed by the hospital pathologists, it was also the case that the number of those types of autopsies had declined significantly in the last decades.

This was a puzzle to many in the academic medical communities, those in private independent practice were well aware of the reason. The families just didn't trust the doctors who were employees of the hospital to render a complete and accurate opinion due to their obvious conflict of interest, which included their interest in maintaining their individual employment status.

"I think the first thing we need to do is find out if there are any similar cases over the last couple of years from this hospital." Lyons responded to the family's inquiry. "I've actually seen several cases from there for which I've done private autopsies, but usually the death seemed to be pretty straight-forward. But I'll admit I didn't always conduct a complete toxicology evaluation."

From the time he started private consulting, including family-requested autopsies, Arthur Lyons had maintained a fairly complete database on his computer. This database, among other things cross-referenced medical records in such a way as to be able to identify the hospital of origin.

Consequently, upon review of the files, it was determined that within the past three years, Lyons had performed five autopsies on patients dying somewhat unexpectedly while under care at that institution.

When performing an autopsy, it was standard procedure for Arthur Lyons to obtain samples of blood and other fluids such as bile and urine when they were available, even though they might ultimately not be tested if there was a clear cause of death determined.

The real problem was that the possibility of inappropriate administration of medication to hasten the natural disease process always existed. It would appear at autopsy to be an uncomplicated natural death, unless some suspicion was raised.

Although the samples gathered at autopsy were not always tested, they were routinely preserved. United Reference Laboratories, where Lyons routinely submitted his toxicology and histology specimens, kept them for up to two years. This meant that they were still available at the time the review was performed.

"Hi, this is Doctor Lyons in Orlando," he began after having been transferred to the toxicology section and connected to one of the technologists who had worked with him for a number of years. "I've got a list of patients, and I was wondering if their samples are still available?"

After providing the names, he was surprised to find that all the blood had been stored, even one patient whom he'd autopsied three years earlier.

"Doctor, we always hang on to your specimens a little longer—just to be on the safe side," she replied.

"That's fantastic! I want to do tox screening on all of them as soon as we can," he replied.

Review of his autopsy reports on all the patients in question showed Dr. Lyons no particular similarities that were immediately obvious. All were hospitalized for various illnesses ranging from chronic lung disease to a fractured hip, had been in hospital for only a few days, and were male patients between the ages of sixty-five and seventy.

Reading further through the medical records trying to find any similarities, Lyons noticed that all of the patients were on a regular floor and ready to be discharged the following day. Then, they suddenly deteriorated and either died there or were transferred to the Intensive Care Unit, having suffered a cardiac arrest, and ultimately died in the unit.

While these patients were clearly not terminal they did have chronic medical conditions that might appear to be more serious than they actually were to anyone not intimately familiar with the actual records. They even appeared to have end-stage disease in some instances.

Further checking the nursing notes, he realized that all the deaths had occurred in the early morning hours. This was the night shift for nursing staff—a time when there was usually fewer personnel around that at other times of the day. All these patients had been discovered either dead in bed or in cardiac arrest.

The records indicated that only two of the five had received any resuscitation, with the others being clearly deceased for at least several hours. One man was even described as "cold and developing rigor mortis," indicating that he'd been dead for at least four to six hours. This raised the question as to the accuracy of the nurses notes that had reported him as "sleeping comfortably" throughout the night, but that wasn't the immediate problem!

Clearly, in those instances, since there had been no resuscitation, there was seemingly no need, at the time, for Lyons to perform any toxicology studies as part of the autopsy. But nonetheless he had, fortunately, collected the samples that were now, even after the fact, going to be analyzed.

"Dr. Lyons, this is Trish in toxicology at United," the call began. "We've completed the screening on your old samples, and they're all positive for Opiates; do you want to quantitate?"

"That's what I was afraid of," the pathologist replied, "and we do need quantitation on all of them—this is totally a surprise."

The initial screening of a sample was really just a preliminary test to give a general idea whether or not there were any drugs in the patient's system. This, then, would direct the pathologist where to proceed further if it was deemed necessary. So, in order to get a definitive result that would identify the specific drug as well as determine the amount present, quantitation testing would need to be performed.

Keeping the Campbell family members in the loop was an important part of the process, so Dr. Lyons had apprised them of finding Fentanyl in that case. He had not mentioned anything about any of the other somewhat disturbing results of the other autopsies. He at least wanted to wait until the final toxicology determinations had been reported.

About two weeks after ordering the further testing, a second call and follow-up FAX from the lab confirmed the presence of significantly elevated levels of Fentanyl in all five of the patients who had initially been signed out as natural deaths.

Clearly, these now appeared to be anything but natural, pointing to overdose, either accidental or—almost inconceivably —intentional!

Previous issues had arisen in Florida involving deaths with high-level medications in Hospice patients. This ended up with a Medical Examiner losing his job in a controversial and very public dispute with politically well-connected organizations dealing with both end-of-life care and pain management.

Arthur Lyons was painfully aware of this situation, having testified on behalf of the Medical Examiner during a subsequent investigation into the circumstances of his firing. This was an investigation by the state Medical Examiner's Commission that not-surprisingly ruled against the Medical Examiner, bowing to the political pressure to keep these cases out of the public eye.

The administration of sometimes near-toxic levels of medications for pain and sedation for comfort measures were part of the routine management of patients in these situations. Still, questions might arise if these toxic levels resulted in the death of the patient as opposed to the patient simply dying as the result of his or her underlying disease.

In the case of this particular Medical Examiner, he found several prominently elevated drug levels in Hospice patients referred to the office because of prior trauma and, consequently, these came under his office's jurisdiction. He became concerned enough to begin ordering autopsies on many of these cases, whereas in most situations these types of deaths would simply be ruled natural causes and not subject to autopsy.

Not only were more autopsies ordered by the Medical Examiner's office, but the evaluation routinely included toxicology testing. The results of these tests turned up the presence of toxic levels of medications in over seventy-five percent of the cases. This prompted the pathologist to begin reporting the cases as overdose, with a designation as either accidental or undetermined.

When these findings began to show up on the Death Certificates, it generated immediate concerns from the families. They demanded to know how this could happen to their loved ones, and threatened lawsuits against the medical-care providers.

As if the furor from the families wasn't enough, the backlash from the politicians in County government, with whom the Medical Examiner had contracted for services, was even more severe. They demanded that the office no longer perform any autopsies on patients from Hospice, as well as cases directly related to pain management clinics. As Dr. Lyons would point out in later testimony: "What the hell does directly-related mean?"

Within two weeks, the County had begun an investigation of the office, leading to allegations that the doctor was "performing private autopsies on county time"—a favorite ploy often used when the politicos wanted to get rid of a Medical Examiner. Despite the lack of any evidence that anything of the sort had ever actually occurred, the County terminated his contract, basically firing him, but with no reference to the toxicology findings that had become so controversial.

There was really no effective way to appeal this action, and although the situation was reviewed by the Medical Examiner's Commission, the State oversight body for Medical Examiners within the State, no actions were taken to challenge the firing.

The upshot of this situation was to impart a chilling effect upon the other doctors in the state so far as even investigating, let alone autopsying, deaths from terminal care facilities. This was a practice that some, in an abundance of caution not to rub-up against the system, extended to any nursing care facility, and in some cases, any hospital deaths other than trauma-related.

These actions, unfortunately, resulted in essentially removing an important aspect of a checks-and-balances function for the evaluation of the quality of medical care. No longer could they discover trends within the system that could potentially be hazardous to the patients.

Because he was independent from any governmental agency, Arthur Lyons was able, as a private practitioner, to essentially call the shots regarding the scope of the investigations performed at the request of families. This included the collection of toxicology samples to be utilized in any suspicious cases, although he would readily admit that the threshold for suspicion was quite variable and completely subjective!

The Hospice death investigation case had had negative effects not only on the Medical Examiners but, to a significant degree, on the State as well. They were often not taking these types of deaths seriously or not pursuing them for fear of making waves, the outcome of which may not be particularly favorable to future careers.

All of this presented somewhat of a quandary for Dr. Lyons. He received the final toxicology report indicating toxic or near-toxic levels of Fentanyl in the blood of all five patients he'd had the lab test, none of whom he had found to have any documentation of the drug being given.

Clearly, if the explanation given in the Campbell case—that it was given prior to intubation as a part of resuscitation from a cardiac arrest—was really true, the presence of the drug in the patients that had never been resuscitated was inexplicable.

Now that the facts were abundantly clear, the next hurdle would be convincing authorities that there was a problem in these cases. He had to raise the possibility of an intentional overdosage administered by one of the medical caregivers—an "angel of death" situation.

The Investigations

"Doc," Larry asked while labelling the blood tubes and histology bottle for an upcoming autopsy case involving a fifty-six-year-old man diagnosed with rapidly progressive dementia. He had been found dead in the group home where he had been residing for the past several months. "How are those overdose cases coming along?"

"So far I've contacted four of the five other families besides the Campbells, and everybody is really surprised about the Fentanyl," Lyons replied, adding, "and they want some answers, but so far we're not getting any!"

"Hell, Doc," Larry observed half-jokingly. "You knew damn well they're going to fight you tooth and nail on this one. These hospitals have too much to lose if they admit they've got somebody helping these folks on to the promised land."

Indeed, one of the first moves Dr. Lyons made after the toxicology came back positive for Fentanyl was to notify the Medical Examiner of the findings. Subsequently he had forwarded the information regarding the lab results along with his autopsy reports on Howard Campbell as well as the other five patients.

These communiques were followed up with several phone conversations with investigators at the office. The doctors always seemed to be tied-up when he called. They ultimately declined to pursue any further investigation, stating that the cases were considered closed, and in any event, did not fall under the jurisdiction of their office.

"You know, Larry," Lyons had remarked. "This Hospice case from years ago has really screwed these guys up! They're scared of their own shadows when it comes to investigating anything that comes out of a hospital or Hospice."

"What do you expect?" Larry responded. "They all saw what happened before! Don't want to end up unemployed! Got kids to put through private schools!"

Lyons laughed half-heartedly. "I guess you're right, but fortunately we don't have to play by their rules, but they surely can complicate everything."

"I always thought they were in business to help and serve the public, not the other way around," Larry observed. "You'd think they'd be the most concerned of anyone that there might be somebody roaming around the hospital poisoning people."

There was quite a history of the so-called 'Angel of Death' cases over the years. They originated in many areas of the world, but probably the best documented, or at least most often discovered, were in the United States and England and involved medical caregivers intentionally injuring, or in some cases even causing death to the patients in their care.

In most of these instances, the deaths were not totally unexpected in that the patients were already in the hospital because of some underlying medical problems, but not necessarily terminal. However, none of the deaths were particularly unusual, and they didn't arouse any suspicions that they might be anything other than natural in manner.

In numerous cases, some members of the medical staffs in either the hospital or the care facilities raised concerns regarding the deaths. The administration essentially ignored them, not really wanting to know if there were any anomalies so far as those outcomes. They feared that any such discoveries could create the adverse publicity that could seriously affect their bottom lines.

Some instances, numerous suspicious deaths had occurred over a period of months or even years before the truth was discovered —if it was ever discovered. The discovery was often the result of an investigation such as an autopsy being conducted on a patient whose death had initially been deemed natural.

Fully aware of this scenario, Arthur Lyons pressed ahead with his own independent investigation, despite the impediments being thrown up along the way. These impediments came particularly from the hospital where all six deaths had occurred. They had their lawyers contact him inquiring as to the reason the additional records had been requested. These requests were to be sure he had the complete records, although most were still available electronically in his individual case files.

"Dr. Lyons," said the attorney identifying himself as representing the hospital administration. "You do realize that these records are confidential and protected by law," he continued.

"Thank you for the information, but I've been practicing for almost thirty years and am pretty well acquainted with the rules. And we did get the ok's from all the families involved, you know," was the pathologist's response.

"Just wanted to touch base, Doc," the attorney continued, "wondering if there were any issues."

Arthur Lyons readily recognized the call to be a combination of intimidation and a fishing expedition. He was even a little amused considering the difficulties the hospital had thrown up in their attempts to get the records in the first place. And now they were beginning to get concerned about the character of actions they perceived to be an investigation.

One of the issues Lyons faced was that in several cases the levels of the drug were toxic but not necessarily lethal. While it was sufficient to exacerbate respiratory issues in an already compromised patient—resulting ultimately in death—an argument could be raised as to whether or not the Fentanyl had actually caused the death. Or, was it the result of the underlying natural disease?

As it turns out, this type of argument would often come up, in his experience, when dealing with both the Prosecutors and Medical Examiners in many jurisdictions. It usually involved cases they really just didn't want to pursue—possibly, indeed probably—for fear of re-igniting the political debates of several years before and raising the ire of vested interests in the healthcare industry.

Larry had pointed out another interesting and frightening reality as he was opening the skull of the man with dementia. "Doc, they're getting all bent out of shape 'cause you found a couple of overdose cases, but how many others are out there that nobody ever found out about?"

"Great question, Larry," Lyons responded, suddenly stopping as he examined the underside of the brain now laying on the cutting board and observing a large silver-colored mass pressing against the right cerebral hemisphere. "Oh my god, would you look at this," he said, pointing to the tumor. "They thought this guy had Alzheimer's, but he had a brain tumor, and a meningioma at that. It could have been easily resected—that's a real screw-up!"

This particular tumor grew from the protective coverings of the brain and inside lining of the skull, the meninges, and were a not-uncommon cause of neurological symptoms. It was not usually anything that could present as dementia, but in this instance had caused some blood flow problems to the brain—with subsequent cognitive difficulties.

It was particularly concerning that this man had died of this in the age of CAT scans. Apparently the immediate cause of death was a seizure that had been initiated by the area of brain tissue injured by the expanding tumor.

Turning his attention back to Larry's original question, the pathologist observed that, "These types of overdose cases could go on for years, you know, because nobody really wants to know; it could be devastating to their bottom line. People won't want to come to their hospital if this ever gets out—they've got to keep it quiet!"

"That's the usual bullshit," Larry retorted. "If they really gave a damn about the patients, they'd be going all-out to find out the truth!"

"Maybe they will if we just find the right people to tell," Lyons replied.

In that vein, Arthur Lyons had decided to forgo the usual hierarchy existing in the governmental organizations. Seeing that his initial reporting to the Medical Examiner had been unheeded, he sent a report of his findings, followed up by a telephone conversation, to both the Governor as well as the State Attorney General—with a caveat that this was an important issue that might need to be conveyed to the press in light of public interest.

Apparently the "conveyed to the press in light of public interest" phraseology invoked enough angst among the politicians, including the prosecutors who took the signal from the Attorney General's Office, that they somewhat reluctantly began an investigation into the cases that Dr. Lyons had presented them.

Nearly two months had transpired when Dr. Lyons had his first contact with anyone associated with the on-going inquiry. It was in the form of a phone call from an assistant lawyer at the Attorney General's office, Sharon De Vries.

"Dr. Lyons," she began after introducing herself. "I wanted to touch base with you as regards to our investigation of these possible overdose deaths and get your thoughts as a forensic pathologist about how all of this could have happened."

Thinking to himself that this was like the blind leading the blind, the doctor responded, "This is a situation that is hopefully somewhat unique in that we have someone within the hospital itself, who has access to all the medications, giving overdoses that weren't ever detected to god knows how many patients."

The attorney responded that she was newly hired in her State position, and she had been assigned this case but wasn't really sure about how to proceed.

"But, Doctor Lyons," she reiterated, "I do want to get to the bottom of this. I may be a "new-bee," but I'm not brain-dead!"

Lyons was buoyed by this somewhat refreshing approach from a lawyer. It was obvious that she had not yet been tainted by the bureaucratic pressures that would eventually jade her views of the office allegedly pursuing the goal of finding the truth. How long would it be before she would want to conform with the now universal goal of winning the case, regardless of the facts that might stand in the way of this goal.

The investigation was formally launched into the deaths with relatively little fanfare and virtually no news coverage, as the State attorney was keeping the issue "close to the vest." This was purportedly for the purpose of not alerting anyone that might be involved in the situation, a move that was supported by all involved parties.

And although Lyons had encountered some considerable resistance previously, the spectre of the State now being involved had changed the equation. This resulted in the Hospital bending over backwards to accommodate, while all the while positioning themselves to avoid any potential liability in the event some criminal activity was discovered.

There was actually a surprising degree of urgency displayed in the ensuing investigation. The State apparently recognized the potential of a mass homicide in which they had no idea of the scope, or even the existence, of such an event. The political fall-out could be catastrophic!

Sharon De Vries really had gotten the ball rolling early on. She had commenced an investigation without really informing her higher-ups that there was even going to be an investigation, until it was well under-way.

"This is really unusual Doc," Larry noticed. "How did this girl get this started so quick and nobody noticed? She caught 'em with their pants down!"

Solving the Puzzle

Despite his initial misgivings, Arthur Lyons was now actively involved in the investigation. Sharon De Vries kept him abreast of all the recent developments in the case, despite the undercurrent of concern from some people in the office regarding his inclusion in the operation. His inclusion that previously had always been welcomed when he was a Medical Examiner in their jurisdiction.

In his initial records review, Dr. Lyons was actually able to pinpoint the most likely times at which the fatal doses were administered. He could now correlate that data, in conjunction with time sheets from the hospital, with personnel records now obtainable through law enforcement. This led to pinpointing a group of five individuals who had contact with the patients in question around the time they died.

One of the obstacles to criminal prosecution was that while the drug levels were sufficient to cause respiratory distress in somewhat compromised patients, those amounts were not in and of themselves what would be considered a fatal dose.

Lyons had recognized that this would be a situation not immediately evident to someone not well-versed with medical knowledge. The drug itself didn't immediately cause the death, but rather it set in motion a sequence of events that would ultimately end up with the patient dying.

While the physiology wasn't that complicated in and of itself, the fact that it required at a minimum some explanation created a potential opportunity for opposing counsel to create confusion when presenting the information to the jury.

And in this regard, he had considerable experience translating the scientific jargon into terms the average non-medically trained person could understand. This was very important but underestimated skill for a forensic scientist whose specific role in the courtroom setting is precisely that!

The problem that Arthur Lyons most often encountered, surprisingly to those outside the medicolegal community, was the resistance from the State prosecutors to sometimes even bring cases to trial where they felt the scientific evidence was sufficiently complicated. They were concerned specifically with the challenge of explaining it to the jury. This was a concern that became more acute as more and more forensic pathologists didn't seem to be able to execute this task effectively.

Since he'd gone into private practice, most of his involvement in criminal cases had been in conjunction with defense. This owed to the fact that, at least in situations involving a death, the State would utilize their own Medical Examiner. Their Medical Examiner had, for the most part, been involved in the determination of cause and manner of death.

The present situation was a little unusual because Dr. Lyons was actually functionally a part of the prosecutor's investigation in contradistinction to his usual role as defense consultant, at least in criminal cases. But it was a very reminiscent of his days as the Medical Examiner.

Many scientists in the area of forensic analysis were accustomed to presenting their findings in terms readily understood by their peers, but virtually unintelligible to almost everyone else. In most cases, they failed to recognize this disconnect.

Consequently, this potential for sowing confusion rather than helpful data to support a legal theory in the courtroom led to much of the reluctance, from attorneys on both sides of a case, to avoid scientific testimony as far as possible.

The necessity to present findings in a way that the average person could understand was a concept Arthur Lyons had recognized early on in his training. He was fortunate enough to be mentored by several pragmatic pathologists who treated forensic pathology as the practice of medicine—wherein the importance of communication with the patient was critical—rather than an extended branch of law enforcement.

"Dr. Lyons," came the call from Sharon De Vries. "I see a problem with this overdose and toxic levels thing in these cases. I can see why they didn't want to prosecute."

"Ms. De Vries," Lyons responded. "I really think we can educate the jurors about how the drugs contributed to respiratory failure and how that led to death. After all, the medications given hadn't been prescribed for these patients in the first place."

Although the attorneys needed a little hand-holding during the process, the investigation did continue at a rapid pace. They ultimately narrowed the field of suspects and focused on a group of three nursing assistants who had been determined to be working somewhere in the hospital at the time these patients suffered what turned out to be their terminal events.

Many personnel, including the suspect individuals, had been questioned over the period of three weeks following the inception of the investigation. Consequently, the rumor mill around the hospital was working over-time. At the same time the administrators were attempting to keep the lid on any adverse publicity that might result from the possible criminal activities on the part of one or more of their medical staff.

At some point during the three weeks, the local State Attorney's office, having been alerted to the fact that the Attorney General's investigation had come up with some potentially explosive findings decided rather hurriedly to become more of an active participant. This was primarily driven by fear of being seen as "out of the loop" by their own citizenry and suffering the political consequences of that position.

"You know, Doc," De Vries had mentioned to Lyons. "They're not particularly enthusiastic over the fact that you're involved in all this, and I don't quite understand why. You were the Medical Examiner here at some point a while ago, weren't you?"

The pathologist went on to explain that, "many in the prosecutor's offices regarded the Medical Examiner as a member of their team and not as an independent medical scientist. So all was well when you were on their side, but they regarded you as the enemy if you were involved with any work with the other side."

"That's really a shame," De Vries had remarked. "They're losing a lot of good information that way!"

"Back in the old days," the pathologist continued, "the professional duty of the State was to determine the truth, but lately they seemed to have developed the mind-set to 'win the case, the hell with the truth. And that's why we see them just cherry-picking the facts that might help them win and either ignoring or covering-up any other evidence. That includes trying to disparage and discredit anyone, including forensic experts, who might try to bring those other facts to light.

Sharon De Vries was somewhat surprised by this revelation.

"Well, I haven't ever worked in a criminal prosecutor's office," she continued. "I spent about five years out of law school doing corporate-defense work before I got job with the Attorney General. I worked on his campaign when he ran on the Republican ticket with the Governor and was elected."

Now it was Arthur Lyons' turn to be surprised.

"You're doing a pretty thorough job for somebody that hadn't done much prosecutorial work. But I guess you've spent a lot of time in the courtroom." She nodded affirmatively, reiterating that the whole investigation had been pretty much her own idea! She added that she had discussed the situation with her supervisors but not the Attorney General himself.

Following this conversation, several more weeks passed with no further updates emanating from the Associate Attorney General. The back-and-forth interactions previously experienced seemed to have essentially dried-up. This development, after a few days, became concerning to Dr. Lyons who now began to wonder if someone higher-up the line had decided the investigation wasn't such a good idea.

"I think they've shot down the whole damn'd thing," Larry had pointed out to Lyons. The two were driving to the coast to examine a seventeen-month-old female child who'd died two days after coming into the hospital with a swollen and painful left leg. She had been diagnosed with a blood clot through use of Ultrasonic imaging. The doctors felt this clot had traveled to the lungs as the terminal event—despite this being a very rare occurrence in a child that young.

"I suspect you're right," Lyons responded referring to the Attorney General investigation. "But I'd sure as hell like to know what happened."

The autopsy on the child was to be done at a local funeral home. The family didn't feel the hospital pathologists would be objective if they found anything that might implicate their employer regarding whether or not the patient received appropriate care.

Lyons became somewhat suspicious after viewing the badly swollen thigh on the baby. Because of his forensic experiences' sending up red-flags, he ordered x-rays to be done prior to commencing the dissection.

Since they were at a funeral home, it was necessary to call a mobile radiology service to come to the site and take the films. This resulted in a delay of about two hours before the x-rays would be taken, and they could open the body and start the case. During this time period, Larry Hudson had spent almost an hour on the phone, somewhat unusual for him, and prompting a question when they finally did start the dissection.

"Larry, what have you been up to?" Lyons asked.

"I got some real interesting stuff from my boys at the Medical Examiner's office about our cases that the State's investigating," was the response.

While there was often quite a bit of ego-related animosity generated between Medical Examiner's offices and any previously-employed doctors who had since left those offices, the same did not exist when it involved guys lower down on the totem pole. And consequently, Larry had always maintained close contact with his counterparts and was privy to a lot of information—and gossip—that might not otherwise be available, even in this case, to Arthur Lyons.

"Doc, you're not going to believe this, but a week ago a male nursing assistant was found dead in his apartment with a suicide note, according to my friend at the office. The note was a confession and listing fourteen hospitalized patients that he gave overdoses of Fentanyl to, to give them a dignified death!

"I guess his conscience finally ended up too much for him to handle, and it looks like he OD'd with the same drug he given all those patients!"

"Larry," the doctor responded incredulously. "Those bastards weren't even going to tell us anything? That's just unbelievable!"

"The word I got is that they're really soft-pedaling the case, and not officially making any connection with the hospital deaths, even though this guy was apparently the number one suspect," Larry responded.

Meanwhile, the x-ray tech had finished processing the films of the child's left leg, and Lyons put it up on a view-box. He immediately recognized an area of irregularity to the femur midway between the knee and the thigh with areas of soft tissue swelling. These were all the hallmarks of a fracture, the result of trauma to the area.

Apparently, in the hospital, the doctors had relied upon the ultrasound imaging to make the diagnosis. They never did a simple routine x-ray of the leg—and totally missed the fracture.

"How is that possible?" Larry remarked, also recognizing the pattern on the x-ray that he'd seen hundreds of times as a tech in similar situations. "So much for all this high-tech bullshit. They should have just done a simple old-fashioned x-ray."

As if the day hadn't become complicated enough with the business of the nurse's suicide, the finding of a fracture in such a young child that had not been adequately explained now necessitated a call to the local Medical Examiner. He was only marginally acquainted with him, but he had to report the finding of an injury.

Since the autopsy was almost complete, he and Larry proceeded to complete the dissection, and examined the remaining organs, including the brain. They found no evidence of other areas of injury—recent or remote.

After completing the dissection and collecting tissue samples for later microscopic examination, Lyons met with the investigator who'd been dispatched from the Medical Examiner's office to take the body for further evaluation. This included interaction with law enforcement to determine how the injury might have occurred.

The investigator indicated that he would take the body of the child back to the office, but he didn't need anything else. This allowed Dr. Lyons to take the x-ray films, the digital photos, and the tissue samples including several from the injured bone. He took them in order to complete the evaluation for which he'd been retained by the family.

Immediately upon return to his office, Lyons attempted to make contact with Sharon De Vries to find out what was going on with the Fentanyl cases, only to be told that she had been reassigned to another venue and was unavailable at this time.

In the process of this inquiry he was contacted by the chief investigator from the Medical Examiner where he had just done the autopsy on the injured child. The investigator demanded that he immediately turn over all the tissues and photos he'd taken. He indicated that Lyons had broken the law by doing this autopsy. This case had already been released by that same investigator as not being something they would investigate, and threatened to report him to the medical board.

This particular investigator was well-known around the State as being an ego-maniac who constantly attempted to exert his authority—usually in situations wherein he didn't actually have much, if any, authority. He clearly was antagonistic to the doctors, apparently envious of the fact that they were doctors and he wasn't.

At any rate, Lyons sent all the samples back but was later distressed to find that the Medical Examiner had not done any microscopic sections on those samples initially—requiring him to later insist, with the involvement of an attorney hired by the family, that these studies be done. He provided him with re-cuts of those microscopic slides—further engendering resentment from the office and the chief investigator in particular.

The injury was later determined to be the result of an unreported accidental fall while at a day-care facility. There was a civil lawsuit for lack of proper supervision, but no criminal charges were ever filed.

And while that case had been resolved, many months passed with no word on the Fentanyl cases and no sign of Sharon De Vries.

An Overdose of Reality

It had been increasingly apparent to Arthur Lyons that the inquiry into the deaths of the multiple patients he'd reported to the Attorney General had somehow been circumvented by someone higher on the bureaucratic food-chain. It was apparent there was going to be no further interactions with him regarding the case.

"You know Doc," Larry pointed out as they were discussing the situation. "They are satisfied that they got their man, and now they want this thing to go away as quick and as quiet as possible."

"I guess you're right, Larry," the doctor responded. "I'd just like to know what's going on. I've not even heard back from any of the families in my cases—which is a bit puzzling."

During the State's investigation the autopsy records had been provided to them in order to cross-reference those deaths with the medical records, allowing the pin-pointing of probable suspects. They had never made an absolute connection with any specific individual until the suicide, after which law enforcement considered the case closed.

Lyons had hoped to look at the Medical Examiner's report on rumored suicide that Larry had discovered. But he didn't have any information, such as the name of the deceased, to even ask for the right case.

Larry had obtained, somewhat surreptitiously, a copy of the suicide note, but there was nothing that identified the individual involved. He'd been told that the file was sealed as being under police investigation. Consequently Larry's contact was afraid to release anything else concerning the case.

In these types of potentially high-profile cases, Arthur Lyons knew of more than a few times wherein external interference had been utilized—usually by the political hierarchy—to either spin the findings to minimize public reaction, or to cover up a particular incident entirely.

He'd had a close personal experience during his stint at the Medical Examiner's office. It involved the death of a female college student in her dormitory room, originally determined to be a homicide based upon the findings of hemorrhages in the muscles of the neck and abrasions on tops of the toes of both feet, indicating a struggle.

Before the case was finalized, a hurried meeting between the Chief Medical Examiner at the office along with officials from both the County and this very prestigious College took place. Following the meeting, the manner of death was changed to accidental—implicating the small amount of Marijuana found in her urine drug screen.

The Chief had sought an outside opinion from a non-forensically trained associate pathologist at a neighboring office. He indicated he thought the hemorrhage in the neck was an artifact and the injuries on the toes were suffered while the victim was taking a course in ballet dancing.

The doctor who made the initial homicide determination had her opinion overridden, and for the next year received multiple reprimands about her performance. Her work performance had never been questioned before during the previous ten years of her employment, but she eventually was terminated on the basis of those deficiencies.

The entire professional staff recognized that this termination was totally unjustified and based upon fabricated allegations. But the county administration was essentially behind the entire thing. As a result everyone realized that it was not only futile, but it potentially jeopardized their own careers to publicly come to her defense.

"Dr. Lyons," said the voice on the other end of the phone identifying herself as Irma Levitt, the widow of Steven Levitt, one of his first autopsy overdose cases. "I just wanted to thank you for all you did for us. The hospital lawyer met with us and explained that the situation had been handled, and that while the wrong drug was given it hadn't actually caused Steve's death directly."

"Well, I haven't really been in the loop lately," he responded. "What all happened with the hospital?"

Ms. Levitt went on to explain that the representatives from the hospital had gone over everything with them. They had explained how the death would have occurred anyway, but still they felt responsible to some degree, so they offered her a settlement. "I agreed not to disclose this to anybody, although I felt you were a part of the team."

The pathologist thanked her for the phone call and the information she'd provided, while more and more of the missing pieces were becoming increasingly obvious.

The hospital administration felt that the reputational damage that could result from public disclosure of an "angel of death" in their facility would be catastrophic. Consequently, they quietly approached both local and state politicians to keep the lid on those cases., arguing that the perpetrator was dead after confessing in a suicide note. There could be no further legal action taken anyway.

Adding to the mix, Lyons deduced, probably was the fact that, in most of the cases, the Fentanyl didn't cause the death in and of itself. It only set in motion the cascade of events that did!

"Larry," Lyons remarked as they were beginning the autopsy dissection of a fifty-four-year-old man who had suffered a sudden cardiac event while in the intensive care unit of a hospital on the coast. This had prompted his family to seek an independent autopsy. "What's in the grapevine from your buddies from the ME's office?"

"I just heard that there wasn't any more going to happen. None of the cases on that guy's list are going to be looked at. They're all afraid to even mention it at all," was his reply.

Opening the chest, there wasn't anything that immediately jumped out at them regarding the man they were now beginning to examine.

The heart wasn't particularly enlarged. It was only a few grams more that would be normally expected, but it was a little softer than normal with the ventricles dilated. This was a tell-tale sign of something wrong with the heart muscle, which resulted in decreased ability to pump blood throughout the body.

They had almost completed the exam, finding no other obvious reason for the death of this otherwise healthy gentleman, when Lyons' cellphone rang. Contrary to his usual habit of not interrupting an examination, he answered, putting the call on speaker phone.

"Dr. Lyons," said the woman identifying herself as the widow of the man they were in the process of autopsying. "Have you found anything yet? This is so unexpected."

"The only thing so far is that his heart isn't completely normal, although the coronary arteries are wide open, so he may have had a cardiac arrhythmia. I'm a little surprised about the Do Not Resuscitate notice on his wristband. We don't have any indication that any resuscitation took place.

"What do you mean Do Not Resuscitate?" the wife responded after a long pause, with her voice now shaking. "I never would allow that! He was fine before this, and getting ready to come home!"

Lyons and Larry looked at each other for what seemed to be an eternity, with Larry finally responding, "Oh shit, Doc. Here we go again!"

Case Study #4

The Case of the High Profile Suicide

The Incident

The jail guard raced down the hall after opening the cell door where accused child sex-trafficker and pornography mogul Ira Morganstern had been incarcerated since his arrest nearly five weeks earlier. The guard shouted almost hysterically to "call 911" and pointed back toward the now opened access point, indicating that there was a medical emergency.

The inmate lay motionless on the floor beside the cot in his rather stark cell, consisting of a sink and toilet, with only a small desk and chair as furnishings, and a tile floor with no carpet. A sheet and blanket were on both the upper and lower cots of the bunk-bed, with that of the lower bunk appearing to be in place. This fact would later be documented in the photos taken by the staff after Mr. Morganstern was removed and taken to the nearest medical center by the responding paramedics.

While a sheet was later seen hanging down from the top bunk in the photos, amazingly there were apparently no photos showing the top bunk and how—or if—the sheet was actually attached to some part of the bed.

The responders had found the victim without pulse or blood pressure. The electronic recordings of cardiac activity only showed a pattern that indicated that, while there was still some minimal electrical activity in the heart, the muscle had been sufficiently compromised by the long period of oxygen deprivation as to make restoration of normal blood pressure, and consequently circulation, impossible.

Nevertheless, according to protocol, emergency transport to the nearest hospital had been effected, with the ambulance arriving about ten minutes after departing the jail.

"He's just been down too long," the lead paramedic told the Emergency Room doctor. "We couldn't get any response!"

The Emergency Room doctor agreed, but because they weren't sure of the situation, he decided to institute a full code or resuscitative effort to make sure all possible avenues had been exhausted in trying to save this patient.

In the course of any hospital admission, even in the often-chaotic situation surrounding an acute trauma situation, efforts are made to observe and record any pertinent physical findings. They look particularly for an injury that may potentially impact their subsequent medical therapies and interventions.

The later review of the medical records from the trauma team would show that no significant areas of bruising or abrasions were noted on the body, and although precursory and often subject to some modification, it was nonetheless an objective view of what the trauma doctors actually observed in real-time. There was, at least, no external evidence of trauma to any areas, including the neck.

It was well-known in the community of pathologists performing autopsy examinations in many circumstances involving trauma that the observations by the clinical medical personnel were often inaccurate. After all, they usually didn't have the opportunity to look under the skin at injuries that might not be apparent by just looking from the outside, and often they were mostly focused on treatment of the patient—although the presence of clearly-observable injuries were, for the most part, accurate.

Nonetheless it wasn't unusual for those same personnel to give definitive statements about their observations. This happened particularly in situations where there was a lot of interest—a so-called "high profile" case, to anyone who happened to ask.

And often the distinction between reporting of objective findings and speculation were blurred!

Unfortunately, the general public, including many members of the news media, in order to obtain a scoop and generate a quick —but not necessarily accurate—story, would rely upon those observers' statements as factual. They would thereby, disseminate inaccurate accounts of the particular event to the public.

And in some instances, the damage done by the false information and conclusions is very difficult to reverse even in the face of incontrovertible evidence to the contrary!

Medical Examiner Investigation

Under the laws of most jurisdictions in the country, any death occurring while in the custody of the State, regardless of the circumstances, becomes the province of either the Coroner or the Medical Examiner. Which one would depend upon the specific jurisdiction wherein the death occurred.

In this particular instance, the medico-legal death investigation system was in the hands of a properly trained and certified forensic pathologist. This was as opposed to a large number of jurisdictions around the country wherein an elected Coroner' might be an individual with no medical training—the only qualifications being twenty-one years of age and never convicted of a felony.

The body arrived at the autopsy suite within an hour or two after being pronounced dead. Because it was still in the early afternoon, and the death involved a high-profile case, the on-call pathologist, Doctor Jason Stevens—being that the death involved a high-profile individual—was recruited to perform the examination that same afternoon. He was assigned the case despite the fact that he was a relatively inexperienced practitioner having been out of residency training for a little over a year.

Meanwhile, the Medical Examiner's office was notified by an attorney representing the family of the deceased that they had hired a pathologist from out of town to participate in the exam. He would be flying in from Florida late that evening, and they requested that the autopsy be slightly delayed to accommodate his travel schedule.

The autopsy was finally begun at about nine o'clock the next morning. Over the next forty-five minutes or so it was uneventful, until a telephone call from the chief Medical Examiner, Carla DeSantis, was piped into the morgue.

"Jason," she asked. "What is going on with the Morgenstern autopsy?"

"Well," he replied, "all the pictures and the measurements are done, and we're about to open the chest and abdomen. Hopefully we'll be starting on the head in a few minutes."

"Hold off on any further dissections until I get there," was the instruction from the chief who was now on her way back to the office from her vacation cabin in the nearby Catskills. She had apparently received some communication from the law enforcement agency investigating the death.

Between the time of Morganstern's death and the commencement of the autopsy, significant communications had ensued, involving lawyers for the estate as well as various law-enforcement entities. The result was a decision to have an independent pathologist attend the autopsy in order to ensure some degree of neutrality in a process that to some, at least, had the appearance of bias.

The family of the deceased had informed the Medical Examiner that they had retained the services of Dr. Arthur Lyons, a well-known forensic pathologist, to attend the autopsy. He was to participate in the evaluation of the presence or absence of injuries, and ultimately participate in the determination of the cause and manner of death.

Arthur Lyons had grownup in New Zealand and subsequently trained as a medical doctor attending Medical School in Auckland. Afterward, he emigrated to America and specialized in Pathology at the Massachusetts General Hospital and Harvard University Medical School, considered by many to be one of the premier training programs in the United States.

He had chosen Pathology, a specialty considered to be the basic science of medicine—translated as the "study of disease"—because his bent was more toward the science of medicine than for the "art" of the clinical practice of the craft.

Although he had enjoyed the interactions with patients in making clinical evaluations and diagnoses, he preferred using the relatively exact analysis of tissue and laboratory data that was the backbone of Pathology. He particularly enjoyed the use of the microscope in arriving at the tissue diagnosis of disease and the consequences of injury.

Following the completion of his standard residency training in Pathology, Lyons became interested in the application of medical information to the legal system. Consequently, he decided to engage in further training in Forensic Pathology—spending an additional year of training in the Coroner's office in Los Angeles. While keeping a very busy schedule at various County Medical Examiner's offices, Lyons had followed his interest in advancing the practice from simply being a spokesperson for the State Prosecution, to a more comprehensive use of scientific evidentiary principles in the courtroom, becoming involved in cases outside the office.

Because he was a stickler for scientific integrity, Lyons had, on more than a few occasions, butted heads with the powers-that-be in the County. This includes disagreements with the administration and the police over decisions he had made when the autopsy findings didn't support either the investigator's theory of what supposedly happened to cause the death of the person or persons in question, or the attorney's basis for a criminal prosecution.

The prosecutorial team, in many jurisdictions, was accustomed to the Medical Examiner quietly acquiescing to their opinions and parroting those to the jury during the prosecution of a case—usually a homicide. There often developed a palpable uneasiness when a doctor would approach the case as a medical scientist, demanding hard forensic data rather than simple speculation.

And sometimes the forensic evidence ran contrary to what the police and prosecutors were presenting to the jury. It created animosity when the doctor didn't automatically accept the role of 'their boy'—a situation that Arthur Lyons had confronted and resisted throughout his entire career.

The Forensic Autopsy

Since Arthur Lyons had become somewhat of a champion in the promotion of integrity within the forensic pathology community, many attorneys in particular had come to recognize him and respect his opinions. This ultimately results in them requesting his involvement in a variety of legal cases—both in the criminal and civil arenas.

It was most likely this reputation that had led him to the autopsy room at the Manhattan Medical Examiner's office at the bequest of lawyers representing Ira Morganstern. He was called in to observe and, if necessary, participate in the autopsy of their client who had just died in custody under somewhat suspicious circumstances.

Although it is often the impression held by the general public that science, and forensic science in particular is a purely objective discipline wherein irrefutable facts are utilized by totally unbiased scientists to generate completely objective conclusions, that perception is not entirely accurate. This is because human beings ultimately interpret these facts, and consequently there is always room for subjective interpretation. The potential for the introduction of bias that may affect the scientific validity of the process.

That possibility was immediately brought to bear while Dr. Lyons was observing the initial stages of the autopsy wherein the Medical Examiner assigned to the case, exposed the neck organs. He did this by reflecting the upper part of the standard "Y" shaped incision toward the head, allowing visualization of the muscles of the neck and the larynx and surrounding soft tissues.

Instead of the typical focal vascular congestion with minimal tissue damage typically found in a suicidal hanging—when a relatively gentle but prolonged pressure is exerted on the neck as an individual slowly collapses with a ligature around the neck—Lyons observed severe hemorrhage in both the musculature and the soft tissues immediately adjacent to the main structures of the larynx. He also observed hemorrhage on the thyroid gland that abutted the upper portions of the main windpipe, the trachea.

At this point the process came to a halt, with the doctor explaining that they were notified that they needed to wait for another pathologist to arrive who was also consulting on this case.

The consultant pathologist turned out to be Dr. Carla DeSantis, the Chief Medical Examiner for the office. She had apparently been previously notified of the death of this high-profile individual and had now arrived at the facility—presumably to take charge. She took over the dissection from the more junior pathologist who had begun the examination.

Arthur Lyons had met the Chief Medical Examiner on several previous occasions at professional meetings. He presuming this to be a collegial encounter approached the autopsy table and asked, "Carla, what's with all the hemorrhage and soft tissue injury for a simple suicidal hanging?"

As Dr. Lyons approached for a closer look. Dr. DeSantis, who until that moment had not been informed that an outside pathologist would be attending the autopsy—something that she would have most likely vetoed had she known in advance—cautioned him to remember that he was there simply as an observer. He was not to interfere with any part of the procedure or take any notes or photos to document the findings.

"Dr. DeSantis," Lyons responded, "I was directed by the family to not only observe but also to participate in the examination as I'm sure you understand fully!"

"Well, you're not licensed in New York to practice medicine, so you'd better just watch—and at a distance!" was the response.

At this point, the somewhat strained professional relationship between Arthur Lyons and Carla DeSantis had deteriorated to the point that there was little further communication between the two. Lyons would later acknowledge that it had been at least partly his fault for presuming that she would have had prior notification of his attendance by her staff. But she didn't hinder his observations of the significant injuries to the neck, including fracture of the major cartilages of the larynx—the hallmark of a traumatic compressive neck injury, usually the result of external forces providing the compression, most likely a homicidal strangulation.

As the dissection progressed, the muscles of the neck were systematically examined and the larynx removed. The major injuries were photographed and documented in the notes, all of which was clearly recognized as a meticulous and thorough evaluation of the neck injuries.

The autopsy evaluation of the structures of the neck essentially involves examination of the muscles and soft tissues of the neck and then removing the structures from the front. Subsequently, the pathologist dissects both the cartilaginous structures that form the actual larynx, as well as the adjacent structures including the thyroid gland, major blood vessels, and soft tissues. This will document either the presence or absence of any significant trauma to the area, as would be present in a strangulation or possible hanging, depending upon the severity of the injury.

Generally speaking, suicidal hangings involve a situation wherein there is a relatively slow application of pressure to the neck. The subject tends to avoid any significant pain, preferring to simply 'go to sleep,' so there is usually minimal, if any, demonstrable trauma to the neck or adjacent structures.

The observations made by Arthur Lyons that areas of significant hemorrhage were present in the larynx and soft tissues of the neck area were a clear indication that significant blunt force trauma had occurred—more likely the result of strangulation, rather than a suicidal hanging.

He'd been in similar situations before. The impressions gathered from an initial observation didn't turn out to be in concert with the official findings promulgated by the governmental agency—in this case the Medical Examiner—particularly where a high-profile death was involved. Dr. Lyons wasn't exactly shocked when Carla DeSantis proclaimed that this death was an obvious hanging, and indicated that in her opinion the manner of death was suicide!

At this point, he raised the question of whether or not the significant amount of trauma in the neck organs—as evidenced by the rather prominent hemorrhage—tended to indicate a more violent event than was usually the case in a typical suicidal hanging. But he was essentially ignored. Furthermore, while he was able to observe visually the tissue, he was not given the opportunity to actually perform a hands-on examination by the Medical Examiner.

"Dr. DeSantis," Lyons inquired. "Are you going to take any tissue for microscopic examination from the neck area?"

"I don't think that's really necessary," was the immediate reply. "This looks pretty straight forward to me. He was an accused sex-offender and pornographer who was scared to death to go to jail and decided to end it all before that happened" was the reply. She made a rather hurried exit from the autopsy suite—escorting Arthur Lyons out of the room in the process.

This wasn't the first time he'd encountered being essentially ignored in voicing an opinion while being involved as a consultant in a case. It usually resulted from either ego issues on the part of the pathologist involved, or concerns from someone higher-up on the food chain that the information might prove to be an embarrassment to the governmental agencies involved—or sometimes both!

The issue of ego did sometimes result in erroneous interpretation of the results of a medical legal investigation. Lyons recalled a case where a college student had been charged with the beating death of his girlfriend during a weekend of partying where the drugs had flowed freely. He found a skull fracture clearly evident in the autopsy photos, which the pathologist performing the autopsy refused to acknowledge, ending up with a trial. The concerns from the authorities were that unwanted facts might surface if not suppressed. This reflected a much more serious and potentially dangerous situation.

The general public has always been led to believe that the State agencies, such as police and State attorney's offices, would act both fairly and impartially when investigating potential criminal activity. The truth is that in all too many instances, political pressures—both from the outside as well as within the organization itself—would oft-times unduly influence the investigation, particularly in the case of so-called high-profile incidents involving some prominent individual or individuals.

As a long-time Medical Examiner working within these very systems, Arthur Lyons was keenly aware of the possible complications that could arise from a situation such as the death of Ira Morganstern. His radar told him that this may, indeed, be one of those times.

A Second Look

Following his attendance of the autopsy examination at the Medical Examiner's office, Dr. Lyons was concerned that he had not been allowed to become sufficiently involved in a process in which the family had clearly indicated he was to be an active participant. They had presumed he would be an actual party to any dissections that might occur, and he would document those findings both by notations and actual digital photos.

After meeting with the family following the encounter with the Medical Examiner and enumerating some of his concerns, it was decided that a second autopsy would be performed after the deceased body was released to the funeral home—where the examination would take place.

Because he'd not been allowed to examine the organs—particularly the larynx—Arthur Lyons felt a second look was essential to determine and document the injuries himself. He also wanted to examine several other areas that had not been addressed at the first autopsy.

Of concern were two areas in particular that in addition to the neck organs themselves, might give some clues as to the severity of the trauma. These were the soft tissues of the back of the neck—the posterior cervical area—and the carotid arteries which pass through the neck while supplying blood to the brain.

Both these areas are usually spared from any significant injury during a suicidal hanging because the force is applied primarily to the front and sides of the neck as a victim suffers a rather gradual and steady pressure. Whereas a homicidal strangulation often involves a rapid compression of the entire neck, resulting in tears to the inside lining of the arteries, as well as trauma to the muscles and soft tissues of the back of the neck—both of which had not been examined during the first autopsy.

After Lyons explained his rationale to the family, they agreed —already having serious doubts that the death was a suicide—to allow a second autopsy to be performed. It was to be done immediately after the body was officially released from the Medical Examiner's office—which was expected to be the next day.

Because his practice was in the Central Florida area, he had flown to New York on rather short notice to attend the autopsy and was planning to return the next day. He was sufficiently concerned over the apparent oversights by the Medical Examiner that he agreed to stay an extra day to re-examine the body. He had enlisted the help of a colleague who was a licensed physician in New York to help out in performing a further examination of the body of the deceased.

After about 48 hours however, it was apparent that the Medical Examiner, having discovered that a second autopsy was to be done, had delayed the release of the body to the funeral home where the examination was to be performed. This caused some quick change to the plans, but it still allowed for the procedure to be conducted.

Arthur Lyons and his associates Dr. Marvin Davis, arrived at the funeral home on the Upper West Side at about eight o'clock in the morning. They were told that the body had just been released and was enroute to their location. It arrived about 45 minutes later.

Dr. Davis, although licensed in New York State actually had a Pathology practice in neighboring New Jersey. But he had agreed to be present at the second autopsy because of the concern that Dr. Lyons might be accused of practicing medicine without a license if he actually did the dissection—even though it involved dissection of a previously autopsied individual.

This concern wasn't completely unwarranted as it turned out. In several instances in the recent past, a consulting Forensic Pathologist, after having been called in on a controversial high-profile case from another State, had been accused of illegally practicing medicine in a jurisdiction wherein he or she wasn't licensed.

And in the everyday practice of Pathology, particularly in reading biopsies, second opinions are routinely sought from experts in universities. These second opinions are usually from individuals not formally licensed in the State where the request was generated, but a number of doctors consulting in these politically sensitive cases were prosecuted—although none successfully—for practicing medicine without a license.

Obviously, this was no more than a blatant attempt to prevent outside expertise from being readily accessible to interested parties that wanted to challenge the opinions generated by the State agencies—and in many instances were proved successful.
The experts from the outside simply didn't want to put up with the hassle of dealing with all the nonsense from the bureaucrats. They often declined to become involved even in the face of compelling evidence!

Fortunately, for the family and others involved in the investigation, Arthur Lyons had pretty much figured out the system and the potential impediments that might be encountered in these situations. He negated any potential challenges by involving a colleague whose status couldn't be questioned.

The body of Ira Morganstern arrived essentially unaltered from the condition Lyons had observed during the examination some three days before—at least from the outside. The back of the neck had still not been examined as well as the Carotid arteries, but after sifting through the red biohazard bag containing the organs that had been previously dissected, it was apparent that the larynx and other tissues of the neck were not included in the tissues sent over from the Medical Examiner.

While it was an occasional practice for pathologists to retain a particular organ in-toto, for further evaluation, it most often involved either the heart or the brain. On occasion it might involve the larynx in a strangulation case wherein the doctor simply wanted to further evaluate the possible trauma after the tissue was preserved in formaldehyde—or fixed—in order to take more directed tissue samples.

Consequently, Arthur Lyons wasn't particularly surprised about it, and he simply decided to proceed with the dissection as planned—with Dr. Davis doing the cutting of course!

Since the victim's chest and abdomen had already been opened at the first autopsy, it was only necessary to cut the few stitches used to sew up the skin in order to access the chest and abdominal cavities. During this, the pathologists were busy taking photos to document the procedure.

The carotid arteries were readily accessible and fortunately had not been damaged during the removal of the neck organs during the initial examination at the Medical Examiner's office.

"Arthur," Davis, not being a forensic pathologist, had inquired. "What are we looking for here?"

"Well, if there was severe compression, we might expect damage to the inside of the vessel—something that is more indicative of a homicide that a suicide since the compression is usually more gradual when someone hangs themselves," Lyons replied.

Dr. Davis at this point had begun to open the arteries. He noted irregular areas of intimal tearing on both vessels at about the midpoint of the neck. These areas corresponded to an abrasion on the skin in that area that extended horizontally around ninety percent of the neck—sparing only the very back of the neck area. The abrasion presumably corresponded to the ligature. The investigators had stated that the ligature was a bed sheet which was wrapped around the neck and tied to the upper bunk from which Mr. Morgenstern was suspended. At least that was the story provided by the personnel from the correctional facility.

"This is very interesting," Lyons continued during the dissection that discovered the injuries to the arteries. "Not only do we have a lot of force being applied, but the ligature mark is nearly horizontal. Usually in a hanging it goes from the front of the neck upward to around the ears—after all the guy is 'hanging.' Besides, this mark is only a few centimeters thick, that doesn't suggest something wider."

"Like a bed sheet?" Davis piped in!

"Exactly," Arthur replied. "Now we need to see if there are any injuries to the back of the neck," at which point the body was rolled over. An incision was made to expose the muscles and vertebrae of the posterior cervical region—an area that had not been previously examined at the initial autopsy.

It became obvious as soon as the incision was begun that there was a significant amount of hemorrhage into the muscles and soft tissues—much more than would be expected in a simple suicidal hanging. It was more suggestive of inflicted trauma during an assault.

"Normally," Lyons went on to explain, "you don't find any trauma in this area." He pointed to the rather large areas of bleeding now discernible as the dissection continued." In a suicide because this area isn't affected, but this is unusual even in a strangulation homicide to find this much trauma to the back of the neck."

The autopsy examination continued with dissection of the muscles to the point that the actual bones of the cervical spine could be observed, and the boney structures were sawed open to reveal the underlying spinal cord.

"Well I'll be damned," Davis remarked as the posterior portion of the vertebrae was removed. It revealed a portion of the upper spinal cord that was surrounded by a large amount of hemorrhage —the hallmark of enough force applied to the area to at least create spinal shock if not actual paralysis, thereby rendering the victim completely immobilized. "I sure didn't expect to see this!"

"That's the great thing about forensic practice—you never know just what you're going to find in these exams," Lyons responded exuberantly. "You got to love it!"

It was becoming increasingly apparent to Dr. Lyons that there may indeed be two separate traumas in this case: the compression injuries to the neck organs and blunt force trauma to the back of the neck. The latter was a trauma that could have incapacitated the victim, possibly preceding the application of the ligature that caused the abrasion and the injury to the larynx and carotid arteries.

This most certainly would not be supportive of the determination of suicide by hanging in the death of Ira Morgenstern!

Both Davis and Lyons were taking plenty of photos with their digital cameras to document all the findings. Lyons, out of habit, would frequently air-drop them to his near-by Mac laptop, in order to ensure that all the necessary documentation would be available as the case—now highly suspicious for a Homicide—progressed.

In view of the newly discovered injuries, it was decided by the two pathologists to notify the Medical Examiner before proceeding with any further dissection. But they were told by that office that the case had been closed and they would not be interested in any further participation. Apparently they didn't even want to see the newly discovered injuries!

Marvin Davis, who was not as familiar with the almost universal political intrigue that tended to surround the Medical Examiner whenever a death involved a high-profile individual as was Arthur Lyons, responded in disbelief at the response.

"What the hell was that all about?" he questioned the group clustered around the body on the table. "I thought they were supposed to be investigating this case?"

"Welcome to the real world, Marv," was Lyons' reply. "Their office obviously got the word that this was going to be a suicide—period!"

To a relative outsider like Marvin Davis, the fact that there might be outside political interference in the medical diagnoses made by a forensic pathologist acting in the capacity of Medical Examiner was difficult to digest. Arthur Lyons was all too aware of the problems that might confront the doctor in these types of situations.

As they continued the dissection of the posterior cervical area, it was increasingly obvious that significant trauma was involved.

It was much more that Mr. Morgenstern could have inflicted himself, and it was in a distribution completely apart from those created by the ligature.

All the while, everyone in the room was becoming increasingly suspicious as to what was actually going on in this investigation. In particular, they wondered why the authorities seemed to be totally disinterested in the newly discovered injuries they were observing there at the funeral home.

For Dr. Lyons however, this wasn't his 'first rodeo.' He was well-aware of the considerable pressures that could be applied to a pathologist, whose job and livelihood depended upon his or her maintaining a good relationship with whatever governmental agency controlled the purse-strings. The alternative was the unemployment line!

Pressures could be applied in a number of ways to influence, subtly or otherwise, the final determinations as to the cause and manner of death in many circumstances. Usually these cases did not involve ordinary citizens, whose deaths attracted little attention, but pressure might be applied in the death of a celebrity or any person of some notoriety.

In this particular situation, there had been many rumors and inferences in both political circles. The media had reported that Mr. Morgenstern had extended his pornography empire beyond the virtual and was involved to a significant degree in actual sex trafficking. This world had involved a number of highly placed social and political figures, some of whom occupied some high seats within the federal government.

Consequently, it was no surprise that this death investigation had the potential of becoming a real live cover-up and possible political circus. This is the antithesis of the objective, analytical, independent scientific endeavor that a forensic medical investigation was intended to be!

Intervention

Arthur Lyons and his crew discovered critical pieces of previously overlooked evidence clearly pointing to a sequence of events in Morganstern's death that didn't support a suicide. However, it appeared that the authorities in charge wanted to leave the initial Medical Examiner's diagnosis unchallenged.

The problem now facing them was determining how best to handle the evidence they possessed. They wanted to find a way forward in promulgating their findings to the public arena since the authorities in charge were abdicating their investigative responsibilities.

In the interim period following the autopsy as they were discussing the case in an office at the funeral home, Arthur Lyons' cellphone received a message from the lead investigator at the Medical Examiner's office. They needed to talk to him right away about the extra procedures that were performed and what was found. They indicated that, "you guys may have done something illegal!"

"What the hell are they doing?" Dr. Davis turned to Lyons expressing mild disbelief. "We asked them to come over while the body was opened on the table, and now they're trying to accuse us of something?"

"Well, I guess they must have just realized that we may have found some evidence on the body that they weren't aware of and need to cover their asses," Lyons responded. He said that he had just texted back saying that they were "welcome to come over to the funeral home and see what we'd found." He reminded them that they had already been invited to observe their examination.

The response was another text message indicating that someone from the office would be there within the hour—and not to do anymore work on the case. That didn't present too much of a problem as they had pretty much completed their evaluation, including taking the photos and tissue samples since there had been none obtained during the first autopsy.

Arthur Lyons was a big proponent of doing a complete autopsy. That included looking at tissues under the microscope just as a surgical pathologist would examine a biopsy taken from a patient in order to make a diagnosis such as whether or not a malignancy was present.

Unfortunately, over the recent few years, many forensic pathologists seem to have abandoned the microscope. They were under the mistaken impression that their cases can be better handled by just examining a victim with the naked eye and using the information provided over the phone by those investigating a particular incident.

This somewhat simplistic approach often resulted in failure to obtain information that would become critical in the overall evaluation of a death. This included determining whether an injury was very recent or if the body's response to that injury was present—observable changes only under the microscope. Or, it could have been subtle changes in the brain may have accounted for the bizarre behavior that resulted in the death of the victim in question.

In the Morgenstern case there appeared, at least on the surface, that this was a relatively straight-forward case. Lyons had been surprised too often not to perform the complete evaluation—gathering the data and then arriving at conclusions—rather than the other way around.

In particular he had concerns about how long it might have taken for the actual death to occur following the inflicting of the injury. This was a major concern particularly after the injuries to the back of the cervical spine were discovered.

Consequently, multiple tissue samples had been obtained from the areas of trauma, as well as the lungs. The development or absence of pulmonary edema might indicate the death was sudden as opposed to the somewhat prolonged type that might be expected in a slower, more gradual process of a suicidal hanging.

When the autopsy biopsies are taken, small pieces of the various tissues and organs are cut and placed into plastic holders—or cassettes—which will then be sent to the Histology lab. There, they will be processed and ultimately placed on glass slides and stained in order to be analyzed under the microscope.

Initially they are placed in bottles of formaldehyde in order to fix in the preservative that prevents any deterioration of the tissues. Those two sample-containing bottles were divided equally between Lyons and Davis with the plan that each would process duplicate samples for further analysis.

Although he'd attended the first autopsy at the Medical Examiner's facility, Arthur Lyons had not really met any of the staff there. His visit was viewed more-or-less as an enemy treading on their territory rather than a professional colleague simply trying to determine the facts regarding the death of Ira Morganstern at the request of his family.

An individual arrived at the funeral home announcing that he was Kevin Taylor the Chief Death Investigator from that office. He announced that he was now in charge of this case. Both pathologists were taken a little aback, but politely inquired as to how they could help.

"Who gave you guys permission to examine this body?" Taylor asked as Lyons, having anticipated the question, produced the Autopsy Authorization form signed by the family and witnessed by the director at this funeral home.

"Here is the authorization signed by the next of kin," he replied.

"Well, I don't think you have any legal jurisdiction to be doing this" was the response. Taylor placed a call to his boss, Dr. DeSantis.

For Arthur Lyons, this wasn't his first rodeo. He had had to deal with this type before—a wannabe cop who now, as an "official" death investigator, felt that he finally had some type of authority to boss everybody else involved around. Perhaps it soothed his ego over the fact that he'd flunked out of the police academy a time or two, but now he could feel important.

The pathologist remarked to his colleague, Dr. Davis, that on one occasion an investigator had demanded all his notes, photos and tissue samples after an autopsy. That autopsy had been performed on a twenty-one-year-old with an enlarged spleen following successful chemotherapy for a testicular cancer. He had fallen, striking the left side of his abdomen

The Medical Examiner's office involved had declined to even look at the case as soon as the investigator heard the word cancer.

He never checked any medical records to find that the patient had been completely cured.

When the boy struck his left upper abdomen—at a point directly over the spleen—the capsule was torn and severe hemorrhage ensued, resulting in his dying of hemorrhagic shock.

Arthur Lyons entered the case, again at the family's request. Upon finding the bruise and the ruptured spleen, he notified the Medical Examiner's investigative office, who responded with an investigator going into a tirade demanding to know why an autopsy was being performed.

Since the autopsy was actually performed in Orlando, as Lyons had had the victim transported from the Gulf Coast area for the exam, it took several hours for the Medical Examiner's representative to arrive. By then, the actual dissection was over but the demand had been made for all the data including notes and photos be turned over to the investigator.

Upon meeting with them at the funeral home where the examination had been performed, Lyons was informed that they were considering reporting him to the Medical Licensure Board because he'd done an illegal autopsy. This, of course, was not true, but it gave this particular investigator a chance to act important!

Obviously, nothing was ever reported, but since all the tissue samples were taken, Lyons had to wait until the Medical Examiner's office processed them. They had prepared microscopic slides—after which the office charged him for obtaining re-cuts of those tissues so that he could complete his report for the family! He had fortunately backed up all the autopsy photos on his computer so the investigator had, reluctantly, to accept digital copies of those items.

Taylor, meanwhile, had gotten off the phone with Dr. DeSantis and his tone had changed quite a bit. He apparently realized the he had climbed out onto a limb with all his nonsense, and he now relayed the message from the top that the office would appreciate receiving copies of the tissue slides and any photographs as soon as possible. This was a request to which Dr. Lyons indicated he would be more than happy to comply.

"What an idiot," Davis remarked after Taylor had departed.

"There're a lot of those around," Lyons replied. "But I'm more concerned about how the doctors and the authorities are going to handle the revelation of all this trauma to the back of the neck—or if they're even going to acknowledge it at all!"

"We'll know in a couple of weeks, I guess," was Davis' reply. They left for his lab where they would process the tissue samples with one set of the tissue blocks and slides sent to Lyons in order that both pathologists could analyze them independently. Although Marvin Davis wasn't involved so much in forensic pathology cases, he was excellent in making tissue diagnoses under the microscope—and Lyons was very cognizant of the value of his expertise.

During the entire trip back to Florida though, Lyons kept wondering what the authorities were going to pull this time!

New Revelations

By the time the tissue slides arrived several weeks later, Arthur Lyons had become immersed in several other challenging cases, and had put the Morgenstern issue on the back burner during the interim following his New York experience.

He had been casually following the news media reports generated by all the suspicions and conspiracy theories that abounded after such a high-dollar media event as the death of this very rich guy who turned out to be a criminal sex trafficker. Still Lyons really hadn't paid much attention.

He was, of course, immediately pulled back into focusing on the case when the package containing the slides arrived at the office. He and his forensic technician assistant, Larry Hudson, were finishing up the paperwork related to an autopsy done earlier in the day on a sixteen-year-old boy who, coincidentally, was found hanging from a clothes rack in his bedroom closet.

"Doc," Larry said. "You told me that the guy in New York had a lot of trauma to the neck. But this kid today had a rope mark on the skin but not much in the inside of the neck. That's my idea of what you find when they hang themselves—just sort of ease on down, and go to sleep."

"Larry, your point's well taken, and actually that's why I decided to open the back of the neck too and find out if there was anything there," Lyons replied. He appreciated the fact that his autopsy assistant probably knew as much pathology as the majority of the doctors who did the autopsies—and if he hadn't been Black and had the disadvantage of growing up in rural South Carolina, he would have turned out to be a top-notch pathologist.

One of the major concerns Lyons had in the Morgenstern case was whether the death occurred concurrently with the posterior neck injury, or if there was some time interval between that injury and the compression of the neck. It was the obstruction of the airway that was most certainly the proximate cause of his death.

There were changes particularly in the lung observable under the microscope that can be quite helpful in shedding light on such issues. It is specifically the amount of edema fluid that has accumulated and the loss of the cells lining the air spaces, that suggest a period of decreased oxygenation of the tissues.

Sudden or instantaneous death such as might occur in cases of decapitation or strangulation doesn't allow enough time to pass to allow the development of pulmonary edema. It only can develop over a period of minutes to hours, as the heart begins to fail to properly pump, causing a back-up of fluid into the lung—with the resulting development of pulmonary edema.

The changes that occur when the lung itself suffers from lack of oxygen and the cells lining the airspaces, or alveoli, separate from the membrane that separates the air spaces from the blood containing capillaries. This also doesn't occur when the death is very sudden. It's too quick to allow those changes to take place.

These changes cannot be seen with the naked-eye, and consequently are not recognized by many forensic pathologists who frequently don't even look at tissue under the microscope. Arthur Lyons, because of his background of working in a hospital environment diagnosing biopsies from patients—using the microscope extensively—had become aware of many of these subtle changes that were often very valuable in making diagnoses in his forensic cases.

During the initial Medical Examiner autopsy, no tissue had been taken for microscopic evaluation, although samples were retained in a jar of formaldehyde in the event it might be necessary to examine them later.

Presumably, this is what had happened to the actual larynx which was absent when Drs. Lyons and Davis performed their second autopsy. Although they had sent many requests to the Medical Examiner to have access to the specimen, they had received no response until about two months later. At that time they were told that the tissue had been accidentally destroyed during the routine incineration carried out in disposing of specimens after a period of six months.

Dr. Lyons had warned on several occasions that this type of 'accident' might occur. While he didn't have the actual larynx, he had seen the hemorrhages and fracture of the cartilages during the time he was observing at the Medical Examiner's office. And more importantly, he had taken samples of the areas of hemorrhage in the muscles and soft tissues of the neck surrounding the actual upper airway, as well as the areas of trauma at the back of the neck. Those areas hadn't even been examined initially by Dr. DeSantis.

The analysis of the tissues taken from the back of the neck revealed, under the microscope, that the early stages of the inflammatory reaction—the process by which the body reacts in an effort to protect itself against an extraneous agent by mobilizing defense mechanisms, including inflammatory cells, to an injured area. These inflammatory cells were obvious under the microscope.

Importantly, since the timing of initial stages of inflammation in injured tissues tends to be fairly consistent—the first cells arriving at a site of injury in about 20 minutes—some rough estimation of the timing of an injury can be made through microscopic tissue analysis.

In the case of the Morganstern evaluation, it appeared that the body's first line of defense cells were just arriving at the scene of the injury, the muscles of the neck. This indicated that this trauma was at least three-to-four hours prior to death—a finding that totally contradicted the theory that this was a sudden death as the result of ligature asphyxia from a suicidal hanging.

It seemed that almost every path Lyons followed led to the conclusion that this wasn't a simple suicidal hanging using a bed sheet in jail, but a probable homicide that involved a series of traumatic events. These traumas occurred over a period of possibly several hours—and possibly involved several individuals inflicting the injuries that resulted in the death.

The conclusions were basically inescapable—Morgenstern had been murdered!

Nonetheless, there was the distinct awareness that this was going to be a very problematic situation. This was further reinforced when contacting the family and explaining the situation elicited a rather muted response rather than the activist demeanor displayed a short time before when they were demanding a second autopsy.

Something had changed in the interim!

Arthur Lyons had seen this before. There was an earlier situation wherein a young Black man had been injured during an arrest. It resulted in a fracture of a cervical vertebrae and spinal cord injury caused by a drop-kick to the back of the neck while the victim was being restrained on the ground.

The police denied that this had ever happened and that the death was the result of being thrown around the police van during a rough-ride to the police station. Dr. Lyons had pretty much proven what had happened as the result of his second autopsy and review of all the records and the pertinent radiological studies provided by the attorney for the family of the victim.

And although he had done a thorough objective analysis, including review of all the records and the critically important CT scans showing the injury, he never had the chance to present his findings in any official capacity. The family had suddenly decided against pursuing the case against the officers for a wrongful death.

Lyons would find out much later that the family had been offered, and accepted, a five million dollar settlement from the city, with the proviso that they would not pursue any further action or inquires into the death. And since he had been retained by that same family, there would be little else he could ethically do but sit on the information he had, despite the fact that it proved the exact opposite of the scenario that was being fed to the public regarding the death.

"Isn't it remarkable, Larry," Lyons retorted. "This bullshit reminds me of the Baltimore case," he remarked, after receiving the notice that the Morgenstern family had decided not to pursue the issue any further.

He and Larry had been working on organizing the pictures and the tissue samples from the autopsy they had just completed when Lyons had received the text message informing him that he could stop working on the case. The family had come to a settlement with the authorities regarding the death of Ira Morganstern.

"Doc, you sure as hell can't be surprised by these shenanigans, anymore can you?" was Larry's reply.

"I guess you're right Larry," the pathologist replied. "The almighty Dollar is going to pre-empt everything else in the end, I guess."

"And I can tell you for sure as hell which end we're talking about!" was the immediate reply.

Inconclusive Conclusions

Scientific legal inquiry had been touted, at least over the last century and a half, as the vehicle through which fair and impartial results could be attained in the justice system. This was because of the perceived idea that the objectivity inherent in science could transcend the tendencies toward error introduced when human factors were a part of the equation.

While this was great in theory, it didn't take into account the propensity for direct interference by outside sources—such as politicians in high office—when the results of these objective inquiries posed some sort of a threat to their comfort, or sometimes to their survival!

Arthur Lyons had pretty well figured that out because Ira Morganstern had had some important connections with many people in high places, several of these people had apparently intervened to persuade the family—through the mechanism of a monetary settlement—to abandon any further inquiry into the death.

Lyons experienced frustration resulting from the circumstances that obstructed his efforts to make the new findings from the autopsy available to the public. But he had been given the clear signal from the State and law enforcement that they had no interest in finding out any more information than had been generated by the Medical Examiner.

It was readily apparent that some people in positions of influence were acutely aware of the situation, and they had a significant vested interest in maintaining the determination that Morganstern's death was a suicide. This cemented the fact that any potentially incriminating information he might have possessed would be buried with him!

"Well Doc," Larry had remarked upon reading the email notification from the family that no further work was required, and that the check for all his services was in the mail. "No good deed goes unpunished. But at least you got a nice Christmas present from the deal!"

The pathologist had to acknowledge Larry's rather sage observation with a smile. He knew that he was ethically bound not to release any information without the express permission of the family, who had now directed him to cease any further work on the case.

It would be virtually impossible for him to pursue this any further given the fact that none of the official agencies had shown any interest in any further investigation—or even learning any more factual information.

Lyons had offered to send the District Attorney and the police investigators the report of his findings and the photos from the second autopsy. But he was essentially rebuffed with the response that, "the case was closed," and no further information was required.

And this wasn't by far the first time he'd encountered this situation. Even as a Medical Examiner there had been instances wherein the findings related to a death became problematic to someone in the political establishment. One such instance was the time he was asked to coverup the death of a female inmate arrested on drug possession charges who died after the jail personnel had withheld prescribed medical therapy. Lyons was ordered to amend his findings, and upon refusing to do so, was harassed by those same politicos to the point of his ultimately leaving the County employment and embarking on a private practice. This resulted in a second career for which he was secretly very grateful for being forced into.

"Doc," Larry continued. "You've just got to write a book about this stuff, and maybe if everybody finds out how much bullshit goes on there'll be some changes made!"

Arthur Lyons just smiled…maybe…sometime…

ABOUT THE AUTHOR

William Anderson, M.D. was awarded his Medical Doctor's degree in 1968 from the University of Miami. He received his Residency Training at Strong Memorial Hospital University of Rochester, School of Medicine from 1968-1970 in Anatomic Pathology. He received additional training in Cardiac and Clinical Pathology from 1973-1974 at Duke University School of Medicine. He also studied Forensic and Clinical Pathology at the University of North Carolina School of Medicine at Chapel Hill from 1974-1976.

He has been certified by the American Board of Pathology in 1976 in Anatomic & Forensic Pathology and in 1980 in Clinical Pathology.

His Professional experience includes serving as a Submarine & Diving Medical Officer, US Navy (1970-1972), Assistant Chief Medical Examiner, North Carolina (1974-1976), County Medical Examiner, Durham, N.C. (1973-1974), Associate to the Chief Medical Examiner, Los Angeles, Ca. (1976-1977), Medical Examiner, Cobb & DeKalb Counties, GA (1977-1979), Pathologist & Laboratory Director, Diagnostic Pathology Associates, Atlanta, Ga. (1979-1986). (Anatomic, Clinical & Forensic pathology services to a network of hospitals in north Georgia; director of clinical chemistry), Medical Director & Pathologist, International Clinical Laboratories, Syosset, NY (1986-1987), Forensic Pathologist and Consultant in Pathology & Legal Medicine, Atlanta, GA (1979-1990); (consultant to the Office of the Medical Examiner, Cobb & DeKalb Counties), Consultant in Forensic Pathology & Legal Medicine, (1988-present), Associate Medical Examiner, Collier County, FL; Coroner's Pathologist, Naperville, IL (1988-1990), Consultant in Medical Hazardous Waste Management: Scientific Waste Systems, Atlanta, GA, Deputy Chief Medical Examiner, District 9, Orlando, FL (1990-2002), Medical consultant, Orange County, FL., sexual battery evaluation & treatment, and analysis of injury patterns in child abuse cases (1990-2000), Surgical Pathology & Laboratory Director, Orange County Medical Clinic (1991-1994), Co-Director of Medical Education in Forensic Medicine, Orlando Regional Healthcare System—Trauma Surgery & Emergency Medicine (1991-2002), Director of Forensic Pathology Post-Graduate Training Program, Office of the Medical Examiner, District 9, Orlando, FL (1991-1998), Expert Witness Consultant Program, Dept. of Professional Regulation, State of Florida (1992-present), Pathologist Consultant & Autopsy Service: Central Florida Tissue Bank & TransLife Tissue Bank, Orlando, FL (1992-2004), Pathologist, Office of the Medical Examiner, District 12, Sarasota, FL (2002-2003), Forensic Pathologist, Forensic Dimensions, Orlando, FL (2003-present).

www.ingramcontent.com/pod-product-compliance
Lightning Source LLC
Chambersburg PA
CBHW060947050426
42337CB00052B/1638